THE GREEN ROASTING TIN

VEGAN & VEGETARIAN ONE DISH DINNERS

THE GREEN ROASTING TIN

VEGAN & VEGETARIAN ONE DISH DINNERS

RUKMINI IYER

CONTENTS

> INTRODUCTION   6

VEGAN

1 QUICK   20

2 MEDIUM   54

3 SLOW   80

> INFOGRAPHICS   116

VEGETARIAN

4 QUICK   126

5 MEDIUM   164

6 SLOW   196

> RECIPE PAIRINGS   220

> INDEX   226

INTRODUCTION

This book is divided into two parts, half vegan, half vegetarian. Each chapter is organised by speed, depending on whether you want dinner in 30 minutes, up to 45 minutes, or an hour – so there's something for busy weeknights, as well as lazy weekend cooking. And if you want more inspiration after trying some of the recipes, the infographics in the centre of the book (pages 116–123) are designed to help you build your own tin.

I was brought up in a vegetarian household – often vegan, as southern Indian food tends to be. Other than pizza night, my mother rarely failed to put at least three different types of dish on the table – whether it was rice, spiced potatoes and aubergines, sambhar, carrots and beans in mustard seeds and a peppery tomato rasam, or home-made mushroom quiche, roasted vegetables and a Caprese salad. Given that she worked full-time as a GP, I have no idea how she managed, unless I'm sublimating the memory of a lot of potato waffles and buttery macaroni with grated cheddar (still up there on my list of favourite dinners). Food for dinner parties or birthdays was even better – home-made paneer, blitzed with spices, then formed into koftas, deep-fried and cooked in a rich Mughal tomato and cream sauce, tiny stuffed aubergines, cauliflower cooked with ginger and chilli, and my favourite, pulao rice with cashews and saffron.

Weeknight cooking rarely affords the time for so many dishes, so I've taken the principles of vegetarian cooking learned from home, and applied them to the traybakes in this book. All the dishes are packed with flavour, through spices or fresh herbs and almost always lemon or lime juice (I am considering shares in a citrus farm); and there's a variety of both colour and texture in each dish. Inspired by my mother's Indian cooking, there are a number of oven-roasted curries in the book – rather than slowly frying off onions, then spices, then each vegetable and simmering on the stove for half an hour, I've designed recipes in which everything is roasted in a single layer before adding the sauce, as with the beetroot, chickpea and coconut curry on page 104, which is a favourite among my friends.

Moving west, I've found that orzo and bulgur wheat are all-in-one-tin heroes – add enough stock, layer your vegetables on top and stick in the oven for just 15–20 minutes and you have a balanced dinner that needs nothing more than a glass of wine on the side – try the all-in-one roasted tomato and bay orzo (page 28) and crispy kale and bulgur wheat salad with pomegranates and preserved lemon (page 136).

This book was slightly in danger of becoming the gratin and tart book, because I love both. There aren't many things better than a hot, crisp, breadcrumb-topped gratin – the leek and Puy lentil gratin with a crunchy feta topping (page 178) is outstanding. If you're after comfort food, try the dauphinoise/tartiflette hybrid on page 208.

My boyfriend, recently initiated into the joys of ready-rolled puff pastry, finds it a revelation: unroll, top with vegetables and bake – it's an easy weeknight win. The shallot 'cheese and onion' tart (page 156) and the carrot and taleggio tarte tatin (page 172) are as good for midweek suppers as they are for dinner parties.

For weekends or special occasions, there are dishes which take a little longer in the oven, but are just as low-effort: try the beautiful escalivada – whole roasted aubergines, peppers and tomatoes with almonds (page 88), stuffed mini pumpkins with sage and goat's cheese (page 200) or whole roasted cauliflower with ras el hanout, pearl barley and pomegranate (page 90).

All the recipes are designed to work as stand-alone dinners if you wish – you'll need nothing more than a grain or some greenery for a full meal unless they're already incorporated into the dish. But if you're feeding more people, it's always nice to combine several dishes and share – you'll find suggested recipe pairings at the end of the book, with combinations that I've found work particularly well together. As with my previous book *The Roasting Tin*: chop, kick back and let the oven do the work.

A note on tablespoons: All tablespoons mentioned are the standard 15ml measure. You don't have to be exact when drizzling oil over a tray of vegetables – the amount given in tablespoons is a guideline if you want it – but a 15ml measure is useful for getting the proportions just right for the dressings in this book. All the salt is sea salt flakes.

SIDES

SIDES

Lots of the recipes in this book feature an integral carbohydrate that goes in the tin with everything else – bulgur wheat/pastry/potatoes etc. For those that don't, if you want a grain to bulk the dish out, here's a quick guide to cooking times if you need it – pick one that matches the cooking time for your roasting tin. There are suggestions to jazz them all up at the end of the page. All quantities below serve 4. Serve alone or with one of the flavour mixes below.

5 MINUTES – COUS COUS | PLAIN/WHOLEMEAL: Pop 200g in a bowl, pour 250ml boiling vegetable stock over it, cover with a plate, then leave to stand for 5 minutes. Fluff through with a fork, and serve.

20 MINUTES – QUINOA: Rinse it really well to get rid of the bitterness, tip 240g and 500ml boiling vegetable stock into a saucepan, bring to the boil, then half cover and simmer for 15–17 minutes until the grains have absorbed all the water. Turn off the heat, fluff through and leave to steam, covered, for 5 minutes.

12 MINUTES – QUICK COOK FARRO: I like this, because it has the texture of spelt or pearl barley but only takes a fraction of the time to cook. Put 200g in a large pan of boiling salted water, and simmer for 10–12 minutes. Drain well, and serve.

15 MINUTES – BULGUR WHEAT: For the very rare occasions where I haven't specified sticking the bulgur wheat in the tin with stock and all the vegetables, you can also cook 300g in a large pan of boiling salted water, and simmer for 15 minutes. Drain well, and serve.

11 MINUTES – PASTA: You know the drill, 80–100g per person, chuck it in plenty of boiling salted water, simmer for 9–11 minutes according to the packet instructions, drain well.

20 MINUTES – BASMATI RICE: Here's my top secret – you can cook perfect, fluffy basmati rice every time using – a microwave. I rarely cook it any other way. Rinse 300g basmati rice well in cold water, drain and put in a lidded dish with 600ml boiling water. Cover, then microwave on the medium setting for 13 minutes. Leave to stand for 10 minutes.

40 MINUTES – BROWN/WILD/MIXED RICE: Stick 300g in a large pan of boiling salted water and simmer for 40 minutes until cooked through and slightly al dente. Drain well and serve.

55-60 MINUTES – SPELT AND PEARL BARLEY: These take a bit longer – either simmer 300g in plenty of boiling salted water for 1 hour, or make life easier and pop 300g with 700ml stock in a roasting tin or casserole dish, cover tightly with foil or a lid, then stick in the oven at 180°C fan/200°C for 55 minutes.

FLAVOUR MIXES: A tablespoon of olive oil or butter, a big pinch of salt then pick one two or more from the below and stir it through:

zest and juice of a lemon / finely chopped coriander / finely chopped mint / zest and juice of a lime / toasted cashew nuts / toasted almonds / finely chopped flat leaf parsley / roughly chopped basil / grated ginger / fried Sichuan peppercorns / toasted pine nuts

VEGAN

VEGAN
1 | QUICK

UNDER THIRTY MINUTES
IN THE OVEN

VEGAN | **QUICK**

SWEET DREAMS ARE MADE
OF GREENS

ALL-IN-ONE ROASTED
TOMATO & BAY ORZO
WITH BLACK PEPPER

RAINBOW TABBOULEH
WITH AVOCADO, RADISHES
& POMEGRANATE

QUICK THAI OKRA
WITH OYSTER MUSHROOMS
& COCONUT MILK

ROASTED RED CABBAGE
WITH CRISP GARLIC CROUTONS,
APPLE, RAISINS & LAMB'S LETTUCE

LUNCHBOX PASTA SALAD:
QUICK-ROAST BROCCOLI WITH
OLIVES, SUN-DRIED TOMATOES,
BASIL & PINE NUTS

WHOLE ROASTED CABBAGE
QUARTERS WITH SICHUAN
PEPPER, SESAME & MUSHROOMS

SPICED ROASTED CARROT
& BEAN CURRY

SMOKED TOFU WITH FENNEL,
PAK CHOI & PEANUT SATAY
DRESSING

CRISPY TAMARIND SPROUTS
WITH PEANUTS & SHALLOTS

LIME & CORIANDER MUSHROOMS
WITH PAK CHOI & ASPARAGUS

QUICK COOK LEEK ORZOTTO
WITH ASPARAGUS, HAZELNUTS
& ROCKET

ROSEMARY ROASTED CHICORY
& RADISH SALAD WITH
ASPARAGUS & ORANGE

SWEET DREAMS ARE MADE OF GREENS

Roasted asparagus and avocado pair beautifully with quinoa and an orange tahini dressing in this fresh, light dish that packs plenty of flavour.

Serves: 2
Prep: 10 minutes
Cook: 15 minutes

2 avocados, halved and stoned
150g asparagus
1 clove of garlic, crushed
1 orange, zest only
1 tablespoon olive oil
A good pinch of sea salt
Freshly ground black pepper
40g almonds or hazelnuts
100g spinach, chopped
1 orange, segmented

DRESSING
25g tahini
1 orange, juice only
½ teaspoon sea salt
Freshly ground black pepper

TO SERVE
Cooked quinoa (see page 16
  or buy ready cooked
  vac-packed)

1. Preheat the oven to 180°C fan/200°C/ gas 6. Tip the avocados and asparagus into a roasting tin with the crushed garlic, orange zest, olive oil, salt and pepper, and mix well. Scatter the almonds or hazelnuts into the tin, then transfer to the oven and roast for 15 minutes.

2. Mix the tahini with the orange juice, sea salt and black pepper, adding a little water if needed to make it the consistency of single cream. Taste and adjust the seasoning as needed, then set aside.

3. Once the avocados and asparagus have had 15 minutes, tip the quinoa, chopped spinach and orange segments into the tin. Mix everything well, then drizzle with the dressing and serve hot.

ALL-IN-ONE ROASTED TOMATO & BAY ORZO WITH BLACK PEPPER

This simple dish allows the concentrated flavour of the roasted tomatoes to really infuse into the pasta, packing an intense flavour hit. An elegant, risotto-like dinner.

Serves: 2
Prep: 10 minutes
Cook: 20 minutes

200g orzo
400ml vegetable stock
400g cherry tomatoes on the vine, halved (save the vines)
½ red onion, very finely chopped
2 bay leaves
Freshly ground black pepper
2 teaspoons sea salt
2 tablespoons extra virgin olive oil
A good handful of fresh basil or flat-leaf parsley, chopped

1. Preheat the oven to 180°C fan/200°C/ gas 6. Mix the orzo with the vegetable stock in a deep roasting tin and lay the vines over the top. (The tomato flavour will infuse into the stock.)

2. Arrange the cherry tomatoes in an even layer over the orzo, then scatter with the red onion, bay leaves, plenty of black pepper and 1 teaspoon of sea salt. Transfer to the oven and cook, uncovered, for 20 minutes.

3. As soon as the orzo is cooked (the pasta should be just al dente), remove the vines and stir through the extra virgin olive oil, another teaspoon of sea salt and the herbs. Taste and season with more salt and pepper as needed, and add a little dash more stock if you like. Serve immediately.

RAINBOW TABBOULEH
WITH AVOCADO, RADISHES
& POMEGRANATE

This tabbouleh has rather more bulgur wheat than a traditional version (which is mostly a parsley salad), so think of this as a hybrid. Cooked along with the tomatoes, the bulgur wheat develops a wonderful flavour – a lovely, elegant grain-based dish.

Serves: 2–3
Prep: 15 minutes
Cook: 20 minutes

200g bulgur wheat
250ml boiling vegetable stock
6 small vine tomatoes, finely
   chopped
1 lemon, zest and juice
25g fresh coriander, finely
   chopped
50g fresh flat-leaf parsley,
   finely chopped
1 tablespoon extra virgin
   olive oil
1 teaspoon sea salt
Freshly ground black pepper
4 spring onions, thinly sliced
6 radishes, thinly sliced
1 avocado, thinly sliced
1 pomegranate, seeds only

1. Preheat the oven to 180°C fan/200°C/ gas 6. Mix the bulgur wheat, boiling stock, tomatoes and lemon zest in a roasting tin, then transfer to the oven and cook, uncovered, for 20 minutes.

2. Take the bulgur wheat out of the oven, give it a stir and leave it to steam dry for 5 minutes before stirring through the lemon juice, coriander, parsley, olive oil, salt and black pepper.

3. Taste and adjust the seasoning as needed, then stir in the spring onions and radishes. Top with the avocado and pomegranate seeds and serve warm or at room temperature. This makes excellent lunchbox food for the next day too.

QUICK THAI OKRA
WITH OYSTER MUSHROOMS
& COCONUT MILK

The quick roasted okra lends a wonderful flavour to this dish – on the table in just 30 minutes. Serve with some quick cook noodles or rice.

Serves: 2
Prep: 10 minutes
Cook: 30 minutes

250g okra
125g shiitake mushrooms
1 stick of lemongrass, broken
2 kaffir lime leaves
1 teaspoon sea salt
1 tablespoon sesame or
   vegetable oil
2 cloves of garlic, grated
5cm ginger, grated
2 tablespoons tom yum paste
1 x 400ml tin of coconut milk
100ml water
Soy sauce, to taste
1 red chilli, sliced
3 spring onions, sliced

TO SERVE
Quick cook noodles or rice
   (see page 17)

1. Preheat the oven to 180°C fan/200°C/ gas 6. Mix the okra, mushrooms, lemongrass, lime leaves and salt with the oil in a small roasting tin, then transfer to the oven and roast for 15 minutes.

2. Mix together the garlic, ginger, tom yum paste, coconut milk and water. Once the vegetables have had 15 minutes, pour the coconut mixture over, then return to the oven for a further 15 minutes.

3. Taste and season with soy sauce, scatter over the red chilli and spring onions and serve with rice or quick cook noodles.

ROASTED RED CABBAGE
WITH CRISP GARLIC CROUTONS,
APPLE, RAISINS & LAMB'S LETTUCE

You might not have thought of roasting cabbage leaves before, but they become wonderfully crisp in the oven – think crispy seaweed at a Chinese restaurant. Here, the bright purple leaves combine with garlic croutons, apples and raisins in a lovely light autumnal salad.

Serves: 2
Prep: 10 minutes
Cook: 25 minutes

600g red cabbage, roughly
  chopped into 5cm pieces
150g nice bread (I used olive
  bread), roughly cut into
  2½ cm cubes
1 tablespoon olive oil
2 cloves of garlic, crushed
1 teaspoon sea salt
Freshly ground black pepper
100g lamb's lettuce
  or watercress
1 apple (Braeburn or similar),
  thinly sliced
A couple of handfuls of raisins

DRESSING
½ tablespoon lemon juice
1 teaspoon salt
2 tablespoons extra virgin
  olive oil
Freshly ground black pepper

1. Preheat the oven to 180°C fan/200°C/ gas 6. Separate out the leaves of the chopped red cabbage so that none of them are stuck to each other, then spread them out on a large roasting tray all in one layer, along with the torn bread. Add the olive oil, garlic, salt and black pepper, mix well then transfer to the oven and roast for 25 minutes.

2. Mix all the ingredients for the dressing together, then adjust the salt and lemon juice to taste.

3. Toss the crisp cabbage and croutons with the lamb's lettuce and half the dressing. Scatter over the sliced apple and raisins, pour over the remaining dressing and serve immediately.

LUNCHBOX PASTA SALAD:
QUICK-ROAST BROCCOLI WITH OLIVES,
SUN-DRIED TOMATOES, BASIL & PINE NUTS

I often prefer pasta with just roasted vegetables and plenty of olive oil, rather than with a sauce. This puttanesca style broccoli works perfectly for a filling lunch.

Serves: 2
Prep: 10 minutes
Cook: 25 minutes

1 large head of broccoli,
  cut into small florets
75g pitted black olives
75g sunblush tomatoes
1 tablespoon oil from the
  sunblush tomatoes
½ teaspoon sea salt
200g penne pasta
40g toasted pine nuts
25g fresh basil, roughly
  chopped
1 lemon, zest and juice
2 tablespoons olive oil
Sea salt
Freshly ground black pepper

1. Preheat the oven to 180°C fan/200°C/ gas 6. Mix the broccoli florets, olives, sunblush tomatoes, oil and sea salt in a roasting tin, then transfer to the oven and roast for 15 minutes.

2. Meanwhile, bring a large pan of salted water to the boil, add the penne and cook for 9–11 minutes, or according to the packet instructions, until just al dente. Drain, reserving a few table-spoons of the cooking water.

3. Throw the pine nuts over the broccoli, then return to the oven to roast for a further 10 minutes, until the broccoli is nicely charred and cooked through. Mix immediately with the pasta, basil, lemon zest and juice, olive oil and reserved pasta water.

4. Taste and season as needed with salt and black pepper and serve warm or at room temperature.

WHOLE ROASTED CABBAGE QUARTERS WITH SICHUAN PEPPER, SESAME & MUSHROOMS

Like its fellow brassicas, cabbage becomes wonderfully crispy when roasted in the oven. You definitely want to get hold of some Sichuan peppercorns for this – they are intensely aromatic and absolutely make the dish. Served with rice and a punchy sesame dressing, this is a simple, elegant dinner.

Serves: 2
Prep: 10 minutes
Cook: 25 minutes

1 large sweetheart cabbage
  (the pointy one)
300g shiitake mushrooms
2 tablespoons sesame oil
2 teaspoons sea salt
2 heaped teaspoons Sichuan
  peppercorns, lightly crushed

DRESSING
1 tablespoon soy sauce
1 tablespoon sesame oil
½ red chilli, finely chopped
1 tablespoon rice wine vinegar
2 teaspoons sesame seeds

TO SERVE
White rice (see page 17)

1. Preheat the oven to 200°C fan/220°C/ gas 7. Cut the cabbage into long quarters, keeping the stem intact, and transfer to a roasting tin, cut side up, along with the mushrooms.

2. Drizzle the cabbage and mushrooms with the sesame oil and mix well, making sure you work the oil particularly in between the cut leaves. Scatter each cabbage quarter and the mushrooms with the sea salt and Sichuan peppercorns, then transfer to the oven and roast for 25 minutes.

3. Mix together the soy sauce, sesame oil, red chilli, rice wine vinegar and sesame seeds and set aside.

4. Serve the cabbage and mushrooms hot, with rice and the dressing alongside or drizzled over.

Note: If you can get the reddish Sichuan peppercorns from an oriental supermarket, they're much more flavoursome than those in the supermarket jars.

SPICED ROASTED CARROT & BEAN CURRY

This South Indian style curry is a dry one, made without a gravy so that the vegetables are wonderfully crisp. Serve with coconut yogurt on the side, along with plenty of fluffy white rice.

Serves: 2
Prep: 10 minutes
Cook: 30 minutes

220g carrots, peeled
180g fine green beans, topped and tailed
½ cauliflower, cut into small florets
1 tablespoon vegetable oil
5cm ginger, grated
2 teaspoons mustard seeds
½ teaspoon ground turmeric
½ teaspoon chilli powder
10 curry leaves
2 teaspoons sea salt
1 lemon, juice only

TO SERVE
Basmati rice (see page 16)
4 tablespoons coconut yogurt
A handful of unsalted peanuts

1. Preheat the oven to 200°C fan/220°C/ gas 7. Cut the carrots in half lengthways, then again into long slim strips, about the width of the green beans.

2. Mix the carrots, beans and cauliflower in a large roasting tin with the oil, ginger, spices, curry leaves and salt, then transfer to the oven and roast for 30 minutes.

3. Season with the lemon juice and salt to taste, and serve with basmati rice, yogurt and a handful of unsalted peanuts for crunch.

SMOKED TOFU WITH FENNEL, PAK CHOI & PEANUT SATAY DRESSING

The peanut satay dressing works so well with the crispy smoked tofu and vegetables – and it takes just 10 minutes in the oven. One of my favourite vegan dishes in the book.

Serves: 2
Prep: 10 minutes
Cook: 10 minutes

2 fennel bulbs, thinly sliced
4 pak choi, thinly sliced
2 tablespoons vegetable oil
2 teaspoons sea salt
450g smoked organic tofu,
   cut into small cubes
2 tablespoons cornflour

DRESSING
100g crunchy peanut butter
2 tablespoons soy sauce
2 tablespoons rice wine
   vinegar
2 small cloves of garlic,
   finely grated
2cm ginger, grated
1 red chilli, finely chopped

1. Preheat your grill to max. Spread out the sliced fennel and pak choi in a single layer on a large grill tray and mix with half the oil and salt. Toss the smoked tofu cubes with the cornflour, then with the remaining oil and salt and scatter them over the sliced fennel and pak choi.

2. Transfer to the grill for 5–10 minutes, until the tofu is golden brown and crisp on top and the vegetables have wilted.

3. Meanwhile, mix together the peanut butter, soy sauce, vinegar, garlic, ginger and chilli for the dressing. Taste and adjust the soy sauce as needed.

4. Serve the grilled tofu and vegetables with the peanut dressing alongside.

CRISPY TAMARIND SPROUTS WITH PEANUTS & SHALLOTS

This Indian street food inspired dish combines crispy chickpeas with sprouts and a tamarind dressing. You could go down the full *chaat* route by adding puffed rice and making it more of a snack, but for a filling meal add some flatbreads or naan along with the yogurt.

Serves: 4
Prep: 10 minutes
Cook: 25 minutes

500g Brussels sprouts, halved
200g banana shallots, peeled and halved
1 x 400g tin of chickpeas, drained and rinsed
1 teaspoon ground cumin
1 teaspoon ground coriander
1 teaspoon chilli powder
1 tablespoon vegetable oil
2 teaspoons sea salt

DRESSING
1 tablespoon vegetable oil
1 tablespoon tamarind paste
1 teaspoon brown sugar

TO SERVE
20g salted peanuts, chopped
A handful of fresh coriander, roughly chopped
1 teaspoon each of chaat masala and/or mango powder (optional)
4 tablespoons coconut yogurt
Flatbreads or naan

1. Preheat the oven to 180°C fan/200°C/ gas 6. Mix the sprouts with the shallots, chickpeas, spices, oil and salt in a roasting tin, then transfer to the oven for 25 minutes, until the vegetables are crisp and browned.

2. Meanwhile, mix the oil with the tamarind paste and sugar. Once the vegetables are cooked, toss with the dressing, then scatter over the peanuts, fresh coriander and the chaat masala and/or mango powder, if using. Serve with the yogurt, piled into flatbreads or naan.

Note: The tamarind paste used here is the kind you get at the supermarket in a small own-brand jar – not the very concentrated paste that you get at Asian grocery stores. If using the latter, halve the amount.

LIME & CORIANDER MUSHROOMS WITH PAK CHOI & ASPARAGUS

This is perfect with rice for a light dinner when you're in a hurry. Use the big grill tray that comes as standard in your oven so you can fit all the vegetables into it in one layer.

Serves: 4
Prep: 10 minutes
Cook: 10 minutes

300g mini portobello
   mushrooms
120g shiitake or mixed
   mushrooms
200g asparagus
200g pak choi
2 tablespoons sesame oil
1 teaspoon sea salt

DRESSING
1 lime, zest plus
   2 tablespoons juice
1 tablespoon sesame oil
1 tablespoon soy sauce

TO SERVE
25g fresh coriander,
   roughly chopped
White or jasmine rice
(see page 17)

1. Preheat the grill to max. Spread out the mushrooms, asparagus and pak choi in a single layer on a large grill tray, then add the sesame oil and sea salt and mix well. Transfer to the grill for 5–10 minutes, until the mushrooms are cooked through and the greens have just wilted.

2. Mix the lime zest, juice, sesame oil and soy sauce together and dress the grilled vegetables with it as soon as they come out of the oven. Scatter with fresh coriander and serve with rice.

QUICK COOK LEEK ORZOTTO WITH ASPARAGUS, HAZELNUTS & ROCKET

This is such a pretty spring dish, perfect for a light dinner or weekend lunch with friends – and a good way to use up asparagus if you've overbought in season. Use blanched almonds if you haven't got hazelnuts – you need the crunch to finish off the dish.

Serves: 3–4
Prep: 10 minutes
Cook: 20 minutes

300g orzo
750ml vegetable stock
2 leeks, thinly sliced
400g asparagus, trimmed
  and halved
1 tablespoon olive oil
1 teaspoon sea salt
Freshly ground black pepper
1 lemon, zest and juice
40g hazelnuts
100g rocket, roughly chopped
1–2 tablespoons olive oil

1. Preheat the oven to 180°C fan/200°C/ gas 6. Mix the orzo and vegetable stock in a roasting tin. Rub the leeks and asparagus with the olive oil, salt, black pepper and lemon zest, then scatter all over the orzo along with the hazelnuts.

2. Transfer to the oven for 20 minutes, then stir through the chopped rocket, lemon juice and olive oil. Season as needed with salt, pepper and more lemon juice to taste, then serve hot.

Note: This dish, like most, lives or dies by the seasoning you add at the end – taste and adjust the lemon and salt to your taste until it's just perfect.

ROSEMARY ROASTED CHICORY & RADISH SALAD WITH ASPARAGUS & ORANGE

This is a lovely summer salad – serve with plenty of good crusty bread for a light lunch.

Serves: 2
Prep: 10 minutes
Cook: 30 minutes

4 heads of chicory, halved
200g radishes, halved
100g asparagus
1 tablespoon olive oil
2 sprigs rosemary
Zest of 1 orange plus
    2 tablespoons juice
Freshly ground black pepper
2 teaspoons sea salt
250g cooked vac-packed
    Puy lentils
100g watercress
1 orange, segmented
1 tablespoon extra virgin
    olive oil

1. Preheat the oven to 180°C fan/200°C/ gas 6.

2. Mix the chicory, radishes and asparagus in a roasting tin along with the olive oil, rosemary, orange zest, pepper and 1 teaspoon of sea salt, then transfer to the oven and roast for 30 minutes.

3. Once cooked, stir through the Puy lentils, watercress and orange segments, and dress with the extra virgin olive oil, orange juice and another teaspoon of sea salt. Taste and adjust the seasoning as needed, then serve warm.

Note: You can pop a bowl under the orange as you segment it to collect the juice, and use that for the dressing rather than a new orange.

VEGAN

2 | MEDIUM

UP TO 45 MINUTES
IN THE OVEN

VEGAN | **MEDIUM**

ROASTED TOMATO, RED PEPPER
& ARTICHOKE PANZANELLA
WITH TARRAGON & LEMON

ALL-IN-ONE SWEET POTATO
THAI CURRY

AUBERGINE WITH TOMATOES,
HARISSA & ALMONDS

MISO AUBERGINES WITH TOFU,
SESAME & CHILLI

CRISPY GNOCCHI WITH
MUSHROOMS, SQUASH & SAGE

ROASTED CAULIFLOWER
WITH CHICKPEAS, SPRING GREENS,
LEMON & TAHINI

SQUASH & SPINACH CURRY

OKRA & CHICKPEA CURRY
WITH ALMONDS

CARROT & KALE FATTOUSH: CRISP
PITTA WITH SPICED ROASTED
CARROTS, KALE, DATES & LEMON

ROASTED TOMATO, RED PEPPER & ARTICHOKE PANZANELLA WITH TARRAGON & LEMON

This is a glorious all-in-one warm salad. The sourdough for the panzanella toasts beautifully on top of the roasting tomatoes and red peppers, with added flavour from the artichoke oil – perfect to feed a crowd.

Serves: 4
Prep: 10 minutes
Cook: 35 minutes

800g mixed large vine
   and cherry tomatoes
2 red peppers, roughly chopped
200g jarred artichokes, sliced
2 tablespoons oil from the
   jarred artichokes
2 cloves of garlic, crushed
2-3 sprigs of fresh tarragon,
   leaves only
2 teaspoons sea salt
200g sourdough, torn into
   rough chunks
150g rocket or spinach

DRESSING
1 tablespoon lemon juice
1 tablespoon extra virgin
   olive oil
1 teaspoon sea salt
1 tablespoon finely chopped
   fresh tarragon

1. Preheat your oven to 180°C fan/200°C/ gas 6.

2. Cut the large tomatoes in half and mix them in a roasting tin with the smaller tomatoes, red peppers, artichokes, oil, garlic and tarragon. Season with sea salt, place the roughly torn sourdough on top, then transfer to the oven and roast for 35 minutes.

3. Meanwhile, mix together the lemon juice, extra virgin olive oil, sea salt and finely chopped tarragon.

4. Once the vegetables are cooked, gently stir the dressing through along with the rocket or spinach. Serve hot.

Note: If you can't easily find tarragon, use basil.

ALL-IN-ONE SWEET POTATO THAI CURRY

For me this is the perfect one-pot dish – everything in at the same time, then a gentle, even stint in the oven – like a casserole, but quicker. The flavours of the coconut, lemongrass and chilli really infuse together as it cooks – a comforting, soupy noodle sort of dish.

Serves: 2
Prep: 5 minutes
Cook: 45 minutes

750g sweet potatoes, peeled and cut into 1cm slices
1 stick of lemongrass, broken
5cm ginger, grated
2 cloves of garlic, grated
1 large red chilli, halved lengthways
1 x 400ml tin of coconut milk, stirred
500ml boiling vegetable stock
2 packets of fine straight-to-wok cooked noodles
1 lime, juice only
25g fresh coriander, leaves only

1. Preheat the oven to 180°C fan/200°C/ gas 6.

2. Tip the sweet potatoes, lemongrass, ginger, garlic, chilli, coconut milk and stock into a deep roasting tin or casserole dish, then transfer to the oven and cook, uncovered, for 45 minutes.

3. Prod the sweet potato – it should be soft throughout – then remove the dish from the oven. Immediately add the straight-to-wok noodles and submerge in the liquid. Leave to sit for 5 minutes, then stir in the lime juice.

4. Scatter over the coriander and serve immediately in deep soup bowls.

Note: This dish is going to generate some steam in your oven, so keep your face well back when you open the oven door after 45 minutes. I speak from experience – misty glasses and all.

AUBERGINE WITH TOMATOES, HARISSA & ALMONDS

I could do a whole chapter on roasted aubergines, but as other vegetables are available, I've toned it down. This simple harissa-spiced aubergine dish is wonderfully filling and works perfectly with a bowl of lemony cous cous.

Serves: 4
Prep: 10 minutes
Cook: 45 minutes

2 aubergines, cut into 1cm slices
2½ tablespoons olive oil
20g harissa
1 red onion, sliced into thick
  half-moons
8 large vine tomatoes, halved
1 teaspoon sea salt
40g flaked almonds
25g fresh coriander, chopped

TO SERVE
Cous cous (see page 16)
Vegan yogurt

1. Preheat the oven to 180°C fan/200°C/ gas 6.

2. Lay the aubergine slices in a roasting tin large enough to hold them all in one layer, then brush each side with the harissa and 2 tablespoons of the oil. Mix the red onion with the remaining half tablespoon of olive oil, then scatter it over the aubergines.

3. Tuck the tomato halves around the dish, season everything with sea salt, then transfer to the oven and roast for 30 minutes. Tip over the almonds, then return to the oven for a further 15 minutes, until the aubergines are cooked through.

4. Scatter with the coriander and serve with cous cous and yogurt alongside.

MISO AUBERGINES WITH TOFU, SESAME & CHILLI

Miso aubergines seem to be all the rage at the moment, and with good reason – the flavours work beautifully together. This version adds a punchy sesame and lime dressing to liven up both the aubergines and the crispy tofu. Serve alongside fluffy white rice.

Serves: 4
Prep: 10 minutes
Cook: 45 minutes

2 aubergines, halved
   lengthways
250g firm organic tofu,
   cut into 1.5cm slices
75g miso paste
2 tablespoons sesame oil
2.5cm ginger, grated
2 cloves of garlic, crushed
100g spring greens,
   thickly sliced

DRESSING
1 red chilli, finely chopped
2cm ginger, grated
2 cloves of garlic, grated
2 limes, zest of 1
   and juice of both
2 tablespoons soy sauce
2 tablespoons sesame oil
3 spring onions, thinly sliced

TO SERVE
30g sesame seeds
White rice (see page 17)

1. Preheat the oven to 180°C fan/200°C/ gas 6. Cut deep cross-hatches into each aubergine half, then transfer to a roasting tin along with the tofu.

2. Mix the miso paste with the sesame oil, ginger and garlic, then rub this into everything in the roasting tin. Transfer to the oven and roast for 25 minutes. Then, rub the spring greens with 1 tablespoon of sesame oil, add them to the tin and cook for a further 20 minutes.

3. Meanwhile, mix the chilli, ginger, garlic, lime zest and juice, soy sauce, sesame oil and spring onions together. Tip this dressing over the aubergine and tofu as soon as it comes out of the oven, then scatter with the sesame seeds. Serve hot with rice alongside.

Note: You probably already have your favourite tofu brand – I've found that the 'Tofoo' organic brand from the supermarket works well roasted.

CRISPY GNOCCHI WITH MUSHROOMS, SQUASH & SAGE

This is a lovely autumnal dish. Mushrooms and squash are a great pairing, and the sage brings it all together. Serve with a quick basil dressing for a flavourful dinner on a cold night.

Serves: 2
Prep: 10 minutes
Cook: 35 minutes

500g gnocchi
500g squash, peeled and cut into 1cm cubes
300g baby chestnut mushrooms
3 tablespoons olive oil
20g fresh sage leaves
1 teaspoon sea salt
Freshly ground black pepper

DRESSING
30g fresh basil, very finely chopped
30g pine nuts, finely chopped
3 tablespoons olive oil
1 clove of garlic, finely grated
1 teaspoon sea salt
½ tablespoon lemon juice

1. Preheat the oven to 200°C fan/220°C/gas 7.

2. Put the gnocchi into a large bowl and pour over a kettleful of boiling water. Leave to stand for 2 minutes, then drain well.

3. Mix the gnocchi with the squash, mushrooms, oil and sage leaves in a roasting tin large enough to take everything in one layer. Season well with the salt and black pepper, then transfer to the oven and roast for 35 minutes.

4. Meanwhile, mix the basil, pine nuts, oil, garlic, sea salt and lemon juice together for the dressing, then taste and adjust the seasoning as needed.

5. Serve the crispy gnocchi with the dressing alongside.

ROASTED CAULIFLOWER
WITH CHICKPEAS, SPRING GREENS,
LEMON & TAHINI

Cauliflower was made to be roasted, and the spices in this dish work perfectly with the tahini dressing. Make sure you use a big enough roasting tin, so the cauliflower can crisp up along with the chickpeas. An easy, flavourful dinner.

Serves: 4
Prep: 10 minutes
Cook: 30 minutes

1 large cauliflower,
  cut into large florets
1 x 400g tin of chickpeas,
  drained and rinsed
1 large red onion, quartered
200g spring greens
2 tablespoons olive oil
2 teaspoons ground cumin
2 teaspoons ground coriander
2 teaspoons ground ginger
1 teaspoon smoked paprika
2 teaspoons sea salt

DRESSING
60g tahini
1 lemon, juice only
2 tablespoons olive oil
4 tablespoons water
1 teaspoon sea salt
Freshly ground black pepper

TO SERVE
25g fresh coriander, roughly
  chopped
40g pumpkin seeds, toasted
Warm flatbreads

1. Preheat the oven to 180°C fan/200°C/ gas 6.

2. Tip the cauliflower, chickpeas, red onion and spring greens into a large roasting tin and mix well with the oil, spices and sea salt. Transfer to the oven and roast for 25–30 minutes, until the cauliflower is just cooked through.

3   Meanwhile, mix the tahini with the lemon juice, oil, water, salt and black pepper, adding a little more water as needed to get a nice spoonable consistency. Taste and adjust the salt and lemon juice as needed.

4. Drizzle the dressing over the hot roasted cauliflower, scatter with the coriander and pumpkin seeds and serve with warm flatbreads.

SQUASH & SPINACH CURRY

This is a wonderfully filling curry – serve with fluffy white rice, or naan breads and vegan yogurt.

Serves: 4
Prep: 10 minutes
Cook: 45 minutes

1 medium squash, peeled
  and cut into 1cm chunks
2 white onions, roughly
  chopped
2 cloves of garlic, crushed
5cm ginger, grated
1 red chilli, deseeded and finely
  chopped
2 teaspoons ground cumin
2 teaspoons ground coriander
½ teaspoon ground turmeric
1 tablespoon vegetable oil
2 teaspoons sea salt
180g spinach, roughly chopped
400ml passata
400ml boiling water
1 lemon, juice only
A handful of fresh coriander,
  roughly chopped

1. Preheat the oven to 200°C fan/220°C/ gas 7.

2. Tip the squash and onions into a roasting tin, then mix with the garlic, ginger, chilli, spices, oil and salt. Transfer to the oven and roast for 25 minutes.

3. Stir in the chopped spinach, passata and boiling water, then return to the oven for a further 20 minutes.

4. Taste and season with lemon juice and more salt as needed, then scatter over the coriander and serve with rice or naan bread.

OKRA & CHICKPEA CURRY
WITH ALMONDS

Okra has a reputation for becoming gelatinous in stews or curries, but in this oven-roasted dish it keeps its form perfectly. Serve this warming curry with rice and vegan yogurt.

Serves: 2
Prep: 10 minutes
Cook: 45 minutes

1 tablespoon vegetable oil
1 onion, roughly chopped
250g okra
1 heaped teaspoon ground
   cumin
1 teaspoon ground coriander
½ teaspoon ground turmeric
½ teaspoon chilli
   powder
1 teaspoon smoked paprika
1 teaspoon sea salt
1 x 400g tin of chickpeas,
   drained and rinsed
2 cloves of garlic, grated
1cm ginger, grated
1 x 400g tin of chopped
   tomatoes
200ml water
½ lemon, juice only

TO SERVE
A handful of flaked almonds
A handful of fresh coriander,
   chopped
Basmati rice (see page 17)
Vegan yogurt

1. Preheat the oven to 200°C fan/220°C/ gas 7.

2. Mix the oil, onion, okra, spices, salt and chickpeas in a roasting tin, then transfer to the oven and roast for 20 minutes.

3. Meanwhile, mix the garlic, ginger, tomatoes and water together and set aside.

4. Once the okra has had 20 minutes in the oven, add the spiced tomato water, stir, then return to the oven and cook, uncovered, for 20 minutes.

5. Taste and season as needed with salt and the lemon juice. Scatter over the flaked almonds and coriander and serve hot with rice and yogurt.

CARROT & KALE FATTOUSH: CRISP PITTA WITH SPICED ROASTED CARROTS, KALE, DATES & LEMON

This lovely Middle Eastern inspired crisp bread salad, or fattoush, is packed full of flavour and textural contrasts: sweetness from the carrots and dates, crunch from the toasted pitta bread – heaven. It makes a wonderful light dinner or lunch.

Serves: 2 generously or 2 plus 1 lunchbox
Prep: 10 minutes
Cook: 25 minutes

200g kale, roughly chopped
400g Chantenay carrots, halved
2 cloves of garlic, crushed
1 tablespoon sumac
1 teaspoon sea salt
A good grind of black pepper
3 wholemeal pitta breads, roughly torn
80g lamb's lettuce
250g vac-packed cooked Puy lentils
80g dates, halved
2 tablespoons lemon juice
2 tablespoons extra virgin olive oil

1. Preheat the oven to 180°C fan/200°C/gas 6.

2. Mix the kale and carrots in a roasting tin with the crushed garlic, sumac, salt and black pepper. Scatter over the pitta breads, then transfer to the oven and roast for 40 minutes.

3. Scatter the lamb's lettuce, lentils and dates over the toasted pitta bread, then whisk the lemon juice and extra virgin olive oil together and pour over. Use a couple of big spoons to mix everything together really well and serve immediately.

Note: If you're keeping leftovers for a lunchbox, remove the pitta bread and store it separately from the rest of the salad, so it stays crunchy for the next day.

VEGAN
3 | SLOW

AN HOUR +
IN THE OVEN

VEGAN | **SLOW**

THREE BEAN CHILLI
WITH AVOCADO SALSA

ESCALIVADA: SLOW ROASTED
PEPPERS, AUBERGINES &
TOMATOES WITH A BASIL
& ALMOND DRESSING

WHOLE ROASTED CAULIFLOWER
WITH RAS EL HANOUT, PEARL
BARLEY & POMEGRANATE

ALL-IN-ONE KALE & BORLOTTI
MINESTRONE WITH DITALINI,
CHILLI OIL & PINE NUTS

GADO GADO: INDONESIAN SALAD
WITH WARM POTATOES,
GREEN BEANS, BEANSPROUTS
& PEANUT-COCONUT DRESSING

OVEN BAKED RATATOUILLE:
SLOW COOKED COURGETTE,
AUBERGINE, PEPPERS
& TOMATOES

SWEET POTATO & PARSNIP
TAGINE WITH DATES
& CORIANDER

PERSIAN MUSHROOMS
WITH POMEGRANATE & WALNUTS

GROUNDNUT STEW:
SWEET POTATO IN A
PEANUT & TOMATO SAUCE

GENTLY SPICED PEARL BARLEY
WITH TOMATOES, LEEKS,
DILL & PINE NUTS

BEETROOT, CHICKPEA
& COCONUT CURRY

ALL-IN-ONE STICKY RICE
WITH BROCCOLI, SQUASH,
CHILLI & GINGER

WARMING SWEET POTATO
& MUSHROOM POLENTA
WITH TOMATOES

SIMPLE ALL-IN-ONE DAAL
WITH ROASTED SHALLOTS,
CORIANDER, POMEGRANATE
& CASHEWS

CAPONATA STYLE AUBERGINES
WITH OLIVES, CAPERS
& TOMATOES

THREE BEAN CHILLI
WITH AVOCADO SALSA

This low-effort chilli lets the veg roast in a single layer, before the beans and tomatoes are added to gently cook in the oven. Perfect by itself, it's also lovely alongside the chipotle sweetcorn with squash on page 194.

Serves: 4
Prep: 10 minutes
Cook: 1 hour

250g chestnut mushrooms, quartered
1 onion, roughly chopped
1 red pepper, roughly chopped
2 teaspoons ground coriander
2 teaspoons ground cumin
1 teaspoon chipotle chilli flakes
1 teaspoon smoked paprika
1 teaspoon sea salt
1 tablespoon olive oil
1 x 400g tin of cannellini beans
1 x 400g tin of black beans
1 x 400g tin of red kidney beans
2 x 400g tins of chopped tomatoes
200ml vegetable stock
Coriander leaves, to garnish

SALSA
1 avocado, roughly chopped
1 lime, juice only
½ red onion, finely chopped
1 teaspoon sea salt

TO SERVE
Coconut yogurt
Tortillas or nacho chips

1. Preheat the oven to 180°C fan/200°C/gas 6.

2. Mix the mushrooms, onion and red pepper with the spices, salt and olive oil in a large, deep roasting tin. Transfer to the oven and roast for 25 minutes.

3. Drain and rinse all the beans and add to the tin with the chopped tomatoes and stock. Give everything a good stir, then return to the oven and cook, uncovered, for 35 minutes.

4. Just before the chilli is ready, mix the chopped avocado with the lime juice, red onion and sea salt to taste. Serve the chilli scattered with coriander leaves, with the avocado salsa, and with yogurt and tortillas or nachos alongside.

Note: Watch out for steam once the chilli has finished cooking – stand well back from the oven when you open it.

ESCALIVADA: SLOW ROASTED PEPPERS, AUBERGINES & TOMATOES WITH A BASIL & ALMOND DRESSING

This dish is like sitting in an outdoor café in Spain, and can make the dullest supermarket produce sing. The quantities given are to serve 2 generously, as that'll fit comfortably into a standard roasting tin, but you can easily double this up as part of a veggie feast, and even bring the vegetables to the table whole before 'carving' and dressing them.

Serves: 2–3
Prep: 10 minutes
Cook: 1 hour

2 whole aubergines,
  pricked all over with a fork
3 red pointy peppers
6 large vine tomatoes
1 red onion, quartered
A handful of fresh thyme sprigs
4 large cloves of garlic,
  unpeeled
1 tablespoon olive oil
2 teaspoons sea salt
50g whole almonds
1 tablespoon lemon juice
1 tablespoon extra virgin
  olive oil
25g fresh basil, roughly torn
  or chopped

TO SERVE
Good crusty bread
  or pearl barley (see page 17)

1. Preheat the oven to 180°C fan/200°C/ gas 6. Tip the whole aubergines, red peppers, vine tomatoes, onion, thyme, garlic, olive oil and 1 teaspoon of salt into a large roasting tin, then use your hands to coat everything really well in the oil and salt.

2. Transfer to the oven and roast for 1 hour, chucking the almonds in for the last 10 minutes to toast.

3. Remove the tin from the oven – the veg should be charred all over and very soft when prodded. Rescue the garlic, and leave the rest of the veg to sit while you whisk the lemon juice, extra virgin olive oil and the other teaspoon of sea salt together with the squeezed-out and mashed roasted garlic. Using a knife and fork, remove the inedible tops and stems, then roughly tear the softened vegetables apart.

4. Scatter over the basil and the dressing, then mix really well together. Serve warm, with good crusty bread or pearl barley.

WHOLE ROASTED CAULIFLOWER WITH RAS EL HANOUT, PEARL BARLEY & POMEGRANATE

This is a real showstopper of a dish, either made with a whole cauliflower or four little ones. The pearl barley infuses with the spices, creating a harmonious all-in-one dish.

Serves: 4
Prep: 10 minutes
Cook: 1 hour

300g pearl barley, rinsed
700ml vegetable stock
5cm ginger, grated
1 head of cauliflower
   or 4 mini cauliflowers
2 heaped teaspoons
   ras el hanout
1 teaspoon sea salt
1 clove of garlic, crushed
2 tablespoons olive oil
100g spinach, finely chopped
½ lemon, juice only

TO SERVE
1 pomegranate, seeds only
40g toasted almonds
25g fresh coriander, chopped

Note: You will need extra large foil.

1. Preheat the oven to 160°C fan/180°C/ gas 4. Mix the pearl barley with the vegetable stock and ginger in a deep roasting tin. If using a large cauliflower, remove the leaves from the cauliflower, roughly chop them, then stir them in with the pearl barley.

2. Rub the cauliflower all over with the ras el hanout, sea salt, garlic and 1 tablespoon of olive oil, then place on top of the pearl barley. Cover the tin tightly with foil, then transfer to the oven to cook for 1 hour.

3. Remove the cauliflower from the tin, then stir the spinach, lemon juice and another tablespoon of olive oil through the pearl barley. Season as needed with more salt and lemon juice. Return the cauliflower to the tin, scatter everything with the pomegranate seeds, almonds and chopped coriander and serve hot.

ALL-IN-ONE KALE & BORLOTTI MINESTRONE WITH DITALINI, CHILLI OIL & PINE NUTS

This is a hearty stew for autumn evenings – the pasta will keep absorbing the liquid, so it'll become less sauce-like the longer it sits. You can use any herbs you have lying about – I used basil as it was to hand, but anything with a strong flavour such as rosemary, thyme and oregano will work well.

Serves: 2
Prep: 15 minutes
Cook: 50 minutes

100g ditalini or macaroni
1 onion, roughly chopped
1 small carrot, chopped
1 stick celery, chopped
2 cloves of garlic, crushed
2 teaspoons smoked paprika
1 x 400g tin of chopped
  tomatoes
700ml boiling vegetable stock
1 tablespoon olive oil
1 x 400g tin of borlotti beans,
  drained and rinsed
150g kale, roughly chopped
1 heaped teaspoon sea salt
A good grind of black pepper
A large handful of fresh basil,
  roughly chopped

CHILLI OIL
3 tablespoons olive oil
2 teaspoons chilli flakes

TO SERVE
½ lemon, juice only
A handful of toasted pine nuts
A handful of fresh basil leaves

1. Preheat the oven to 180°C fan/200°C/ gas 6.

2. Mix all the ingredients in a deep-sided roasting tin, then cover tightly with foil, transfer to the oven and cook for 50 minutes.

3. Meanwhile, make the chilli oil. Heat the olive oil in a small pan and add the chilli flakes. Let it bubble over a medium heat for 30 seconds, then take the pan off the heat. Leave the oil to infuse while the minestrone cooks.

4. Remove the roasting tin from the oven and let it sit for 10 minutes, uncovered, then taste and adjust the salt, pepper and lemon juice – you will need plenty of all of them. Serve drizzled with the chilli oil and scattered with the pine nuts and basil leaves.

Note: Chop the carrot and celery as finely as you can so they'll melt into the sauce.

GADO GADO: INDONESIAN SALAD WITH WARM POTATOES, GREEN BEANS, BEANSPROUTS & PEANUT-COCONUT DRESSING

This is probably my favourite dish in the book – roast potatoes with a spicy peanut dressing and green veg – what's not to like? It's been a hit with all my recipe testers too – a potato salad on acid.

Serves: 2
Prep: 15 minutes
Cook: 1 hour

1kg Charlotte potatoes, halved
2 tablespoons olive oil
1 teaspoon sea salt
240g green beans
300g beansprouts
A handful of fresh coriander,
   to serve

DRESSING
50g crunchy peanut butter
80ml coconut milk
2 tablespoons lime juice
1½ tablespoons soy sauce
1 fresh red chilli, grated
2.5cm ginger, grated

1. Preheat the oven to 180°C fan/200°C/ gas 6.

2. Mix the potatoes in a roasting tin with the oil and salt, then transfer to the oven and cook for 40 minutes.

3. Meanwhile, mix together all the ingredients for the dressing. Depending on your brand of peanut butter, you may need to add a little more coconut milk so you have a thick, spoonable dressing consistency. Taste and adjust the seasoning as needed.

4. Once the potatoes have had 40 minutes, add the green beans and beansprouts. Add a splash more oil if needed, then return to the oven for a further 20 minutes.

5. Scatter the potatoes and vegetables with the coriander and serve warm or at room temperature, with the dressing alongside.

    Note: Check the seasoning of the dressing by putting a little bit on a cooked potato, and tasting. Add more soy sauce to the rest of the dressing as needed.

OVEN BAKED RATATOUILLE:
SLOW COOKED COURGETTE,
AUBERGINE, PEPPERS & TOMATOES

The trick with this ratatouille is to cut the courgettes really thinly, so they absorb all the flavours from the sauce. This is lovely on the day it is made, but even better the next day, warmed through in the oven, so if you're in the mood for a spot of batch cooking for the week ahead, this is your dish.

Serves: 4
Prep: 10 minutes
Cook: 1 hour

2 large courgettes,
   very thinly sliced
1 large aubergine, sliced into
   5mm half-moons
2 red peppers, roughly chopped
1 red onion, roughly chopped
2 cloves of garlic, crushed
2 tablespoons olive oil
2 heaped teaspoons sea salt
Freshly ground black pepper
25g fresh basil, roughly
   chopped
2 x 400g tins of chopped
   tomatoes
75g fresh white breadcrumbs
30g vegan parmesan, grated

TO SERVE
Crusty bread

1. Preheat the oven to 180°C fan/200°C/ gas 6.

2. Mix the vegetables, garlic, oil, salt, pepper and basil in a medium-sized roasting tin or lasagne dish, then top with the tinned tomatoes. Smooth the tomatoes over the vegetables, then transfer to the oven and roast for 30 minutes.

3. Remove the tin from the oven and increase the heat to 200°C fan/220°C/ gas 7. Give the vegetables a bit of a stir, then top with the breadcrumbs and parmesan and return to the oven for a further 30 minutes.

4. Leave the ratatouille to cool down for 10–15 minutes, then serve with plenty of crusty bread.

Note: Don't panic if it looks like there's too much liquid in the tin after the first 30 minutes; this absorbs perfectly by the end.

SWEET POTATO & PARSNIP
TAGINE WITH DATES & CORIANDER

Tagines are traditionally 'throw-everything-into-the-pot-and-wait' sort of dishes. By all means use an actual tagine if you have one, but a roasting tin covered in foil works just as well. This is sweet and intense – serve with vegan yogurt and flatbreads or cous cous.

Serves: 4
Prep: 10 minutes
Cook: 1 hour

500g parsnips, peeled
  and cut into 1cm slices
500g sweet potatoes, peeled
  and cut into 1cm half-moons
5 spring onions, finely chopped
2 cloves of garlic, crushed
5cm ginger, grated
1 bay leaf
2 heaped teaspoons
  ras el hanout
1 teaspoon sea salt
10 nice plump dates, halved
400ml passata
400ml vegetable stock
A handful of fresh coriander,
  roughly chopped
A handful of toasted almonds

1. Preheat the oven to 180°C fan/200°C/gas 6.

2. Tip everything except the coriander and the toasted almonds into a roasting tin, mix well, then cover tightly with foil, transfer to the oven and roast for 1 hour.

3. Once cooked, give it another stir and taste for salt – adjust as needed. Scatter over the coriander and toasted almonds and serve hot, with cous cous or flatbreads.

PERSIAN MUSHROOMS
WITH POMEGRANATE
& WALNUTS

This dish is a vegetarian version of my favourite Persian dish, fesenjan stew. There's such an amazing depth of flavour from the pomegranate molasses and ground walnuts – if you have time, it's well worth toasting the walnuts in the oven for 10 minutes before starting the recipe, but if not, this is delicious as it is. Serve with rice or cous cous.

Serves: 4
Prep: 10 minutes
Cook: 45 minutes

600g chestnut mushrooms
2 onions, finely chopped
1 tablespoon olive oil
1 teaspoon sea salt
Freshly ground black pepper
75g walnuts, roughly broken
75ml pomegranate molasses
100ml vegetable stock
1 teaspoon dark brown sugar
1 pomegranate, seeds only
A handful of fresh coriander,
   chopped

1. Preheat the oven to 180°C fan/200°C/ gas 6.

2. Mix the mushrooms, onions, olive oil, salt and pepper in a roasting tin, then transfer to the oven to roast for 20 minutes.

3. Meanwhile, blitz half of the walnuts in a spice grinder (if you have toasted them, let them cool down before blitzing) until finely ground. Mix with the pomegranate molasses, vegetable stock and dark brown sugar. Once the mushrooms have had 20 minutes, stir the pomegranate sauce through, then return to the oven for 25 minutes.

4. Scatter with the remaining walnuts, pomegranate seeds and coriander before serving with rice or cous cous.

GROUNDNUT STEW: SWEET POTATO IN A PEANUT & TOMATO SAUCE

I hadn't had a groundnut stew before trying the one in Ruby Tandoh's *Flavour*, and found the combination of peanut, tomato and chilli in a sauce addictive – it's my most requested dinner at home. This vegan version, with chunky sweet potato and onions, is a good alternative – serve with a bowl of freshly cooked white rice.

Serves: 4
Prep: 10 minutes
Cook: 1 hour

1kg sweet potatoes, peeled
  and cut into 1cm slices
1 onion, roughly sliced
2.5 cm ginger, grated
2 cloves of garlic, crushed
1 Scotch bonnet chilli, pierced
1 tablespoon olive oil
1 teaspoon sea salt
50g peanut butter
1 x 400g tin of chopped
  tomatoes
400ml vegetable stock

TO SERVE
A handful of fresh coriander,
  chopped
A handful of salted peanuts,
  roughly chopped
White rice (see page 17)

1. Preheat the oven to 180°C fan/200°C/ gas 6.

2. Mix the sweet potatoes, onion, ginger, garlic and Scotch bonnet with the oil and salt in a roasting tin, then transfer to the oven and cook for 45 minutes, until the sweet potato is just soft when prodded with a fork.

3. Mix together the peanut butter, chopped tomatoes and vegetable stock, and pour over the roasted sweet potatoes. Give everything a good stir, then return to the oven for a further 15 minutes.

4. Fish out the Scotch bonnet, season to taste with salt and scatter over the chopped coriander and peanuts. Serve with hot rice.

GENTLY SPICED PEARL BARLEY
WITH TOMATOES, LEEKS,
DILL & PINE NUTS

This all-in-one pearl barley dish is like a light risotto: warming and full of flavour. It's smart enough to serve as part of a sharing table for friends, and comforting enough for a TV dinner with a glass of (red) wine and an episode of *Scandal*.

Serves: 4
Prep: 10 minutes
Cook: 1 hour

450g vine tomatoes, chopped
2 leeks, thinly sliced
2 cloves of garlic, grated
1 teaspoon chilli flakes
1 teaspoon sea salt
2 bay leaves
300g pearl barley
700ml vegetable stock
1 tablespoon olive oil
40g pine nuts, toasted

DRESSING
1 tablespoon lemon juice
2 tablespoons extra virgin
  olive oil
1 teaspoon sea salt
Freshly ground black pepper
25g fresh dill, roughly chopped

1. Preheat the oven to 180°C fan/200°C/ gas 6.

2. Mix the tomatoes, leeks, garlic, chilli flakes, salt, bay leaves, pearl barley, stock and olive oil in a deep roasting tin or casserole dish and cover tightly with foil or a lid. Transfer to the oven and cook for 1 hour.

3. Meanwhile, whisk together the lemon juice, extra virgin olive oil, sea salt, black pepper and dill and set aside.

4. Once the pearl barley is cooked, stir through the dill dressing and season to taste with salt, pepper and lemon juice. Serve scattered with the pine nuts.

BEETROOT, CHICKPEA & COCONUT CURRY

Roasted spiced beetroot and chickpeas form the base for this dish, while the coconut milk reduces down quickly in a hot oven to make a simple and delicious curry sauce. Serve with rice or naan bread to create a filling meal.

Serves: 2
Prep: 15 minutes
Cook: 50 minutes

1 onion, roughly chopped
600g beetroot, peeled
   and cut into small wedges
1 x 400g tin of chickpeas,
   drained and rinsed
2 cloves of garlic, crushed
5cm ginger, grated
1 red chilli, roughly chopped
1 heaped teaspoon ground
   cumin
1 heaped teaspoon ground
   coriander
1 heaped teaspoon ground
   ginger
½ teaspoon ground turmeric
1 tablespoon vegetable oil
1 teaspoon sea salt
1 x 400g tin of coconut milk

TO SERVE
Basmati rice (see page 17)
   or naan breads
A handful of fresh coriander
Coconut flakes (optional)

1. Preheat the oven to 180°C fan/200°C/ gas 6.

2. Mix the onion, beetroot and chickpeas in a roasting tin with the garlic, ginger, chilli, spices, oil and salt, then transfer to the oven and roast for 40 minutes.

3. Give the coconut milk a good stir, then pour it over the beetroot and mix well. Return the roasting tin to the oven for 10 minutes.

4. Taste and season with more salt as needed and serve with rice or naan, scattered with fresh coriander and coconut flakes, if using.

Note: You might want to use gloves while you're preparing the beetroot, to avoid stained hands.

ALL-IN-ONE STICKY RICE WITH BROCCOLI, SQUASH, CHILLI & GINGER

This sticky coconut rice works perfectly with the sharp coriander and lime dressing, with a good contrast from the sweetness of the squash and crunch from the cashews. It doubles up easily if you're feeding more people.

Serves: 2
Prep: 10 minutes
Cook: 1 hour

150g jasmine rice
1 x 400ml tin of coconut milk
1 tablespoon soy sauce
2.5cm ginger, grated
1 clove of garlic
300g squash, peeled and cut
   into 1cm cubes
300g broccoli, cut into florets
30g toasted cashews,
   to serve

DRESSING
2 tablespoons sesame oil
2 tablespoons lime juice
2 tablespoons soy sauce
2.5cm ginger, grated
1 red chilli, finely chopped
20g fresh coriander,
   finely chopped

1. Preheat the oven to 180°C fan/200°C/ gas 6.

2. Mix the rice, coconut milk, soy sauce, ginger and garlic in a small roasting tin and top with the squash. Cover tightly with foil, then transfer to the oven and cook for 45 minutes.

3. Top the rice and squash with the broccoli, then re-cover and return to the oven for a final 15 minutes. Pop the cashew nuts into the oven on a small tray to toast at the same time.

4. Mix together the oil, lime juice, soy sauce, ginger, chilli and coriander, adjusting the soy and lime juice to taste.

5. Tip the dressing over the hot broccoli, rice and squash, scatter with the toasted cashews and serve hot.

    Note: Deseed the chilli if you prefer a less hot dressing.

WARMING SWEET POTATO
& MUSHROOM POLENTA
WITH TOMATOES

I hadn't thought polenta could be baked before reading it in Alice Hart's *The New Vegetarian* – it's a wonderful, effort-free way to cook the grain. This recipe is an homage to hers, albeit with garlicky mushrooms and soft, quick roasted tomatoes as a topping.

Serves: 2
Prep: 10 minutes
Cook: 55 minutes

150g polenta
400ml vegetable stock
3 tablespoons olive oil
300g sweet potatoes, peeled
   and cut into 5mm chunks
Freshly ground black pepper
300g mini portobello or
   chestnut mushrooms, sliced
250g cherry tomatoes, halved
2 cloves of garlic, crushed
1 teaspoon sea salt
Freshly ground black pepper

DRESSING
15g fresh flat-leaf parsley,
   finely chopped
1 lemon, juice only
2 tablespoons extra virgin
   olive oil
½ teaspoon chilli flakes

1. Preheat the oven to 180°C fan/200°C/ gas 6.

2. Line a roasting tin with baking paper, then tip in the polenta, vegetable stock, 2 tablespoons of olive oil and the sweet potatoes. Stir, season well with black pepper, then transfer to the oven and cook, uncovered, for 40 minutes.

3. Meanwhile, mix together the parsley, lemon juice, extra virgin olive oil and chilli flakes for the dressing.

4. Stir the mushrooms, tomatoes, garlic, salt, pepper and another tablespoon of olive oil together and set aside.

5. Once the polenta has had 40 minutes, take the tin out of the oven and give it a good stir. Top with the mushroom and tomato mixture and return to the oven for a further 15 minutes, after which the mushrooms should be softened and the polenta crisp. Serve with the dressing alongside and a green salad.

SIMPLE ALL-IN-ONE DAAL
WITH ROASTED SHALLOTS, CORIANDER,
POMEGRANATE & CASHEWS

This easy, flavoursome daal will look after itself in the oven for
an hour, so you won't need to worry about it running dry. With
a little coconut milk or single cream stirred through at the end,
it's rich and comforting – perfect with rice or naan bread.

Serves: 4
Prep: 10 minutes
Cook: 1 hour 25 minutes

250g banana shallots, peeled
   and halved
1 tablespoon vegetable oil
1 bay leaf
1 teaspoon ground cumin
1 teaspoon ground coriander
½ teaspoon ground turmeric
1 teaspoon freshly ground black
   pepper
225g brown lentils, rinsed well
700ml boiling water
5cm ginger, grated
2 cloves of garlic, crushed
2 teaspoons sea salt
150ml coconut milk/single
   cream
1 lime, juice only

TO SERVE
1 pomegranate, seeds only
A handful of fresh coriander,
   roughly chopped
A handful of toasted cashews

1. Preheat the oven to 180°C fan/200°C/
   gas 6.

2. Tip the banana shallots into a small
   deep roasting tin and mix well with
   the vegetable oil, bay leaf and spices.
   Transfer to the oven and roast for 25
   minutes.

3. After 25 minutes, add the rinsed lentils,
   boiling water, ginger and garlic to the
   tin. Give everything a good stir, then
   cover tightly with foil and return to the
   oven for 1 hour.

4. As soon as the lentils have had an hour,
   season generously with the salt and stir
   through the coconut milk or single cream.
   Taste and add lime juice and more salt as
   needed. Scatter over the pomegranate
   seeds, coriander and cashews, and serve
   with rice or naan bread.

CAPONATA STYLE AUBERGINES WITH OLIVES, CAPERS & TOMATOES

This is the sort of dish you could eat straight from the tin – gloriously tomatoey, with so much flavour from the capers and olives. Use baby aubergines if you can get them – if not, ordinary aubergines sliced into eighths work well.

Serves: 4
Prep: 10 minutes
Cook: 1 hour

800g baby aubergines
1 red onion, cut into eighths
2 tablespoons olive oil
2 teaspoons sea salt
2 cloves of garlic, crushed
3 sprigs of fresh rosemary
25g capers
75g pitted green olives
2 x 400g tins of tomatoes
2 teaspoons red wine vinegar
25g fresh basil, torn
30g toasted almonds

TO SERVE
Bulgur wheat (see page 16)
  or focaccia

1. Preheat the oven to 180°C fan/200°C/gas 6.

2. Slice the baby aubergines lengthways, leaving the stems intact, then transfer to a roasting tin along with the onion. Rub everything well with the olive oil, sea salt and garlic and top with the rosemary. Transfer to the oven and roast for 40 minutes.

3. Add the capers, olives, tinned tomatoes and red wine vinegar, stir gently, then return to the oven to cook for a further 20 minutes, until the sauce has reduced down. Taste and adjust the seasoning as needed. Scatter over the torn basil and almonds and serve with bulgur wheat or focaccia.

DRESS

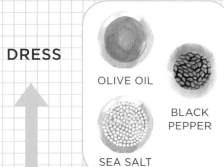

OLIVE OIL

BLACK PEPPER

SEA SALT

+

ACIDITY

LEMON

POMEGRANATE MOLASSES

LIME

VINEGAR

ADD

FRESH

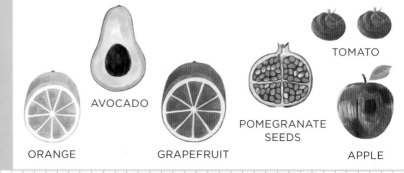

ORANGE

AVOCADO

GRAPEFRUIT

POMEGRANATE SEEDS

TOMATO

APPLE

PROTEIN

ALMONDS

CASHEWS

GOAT'S CHEESE

GORGONZOLA PICCANTE

FETA

ROAST

OLIVE OIL

SEA SALT

+

VEG

CELERIAC

BEETROOT

BUTTERNUT SQUASH

HERBS

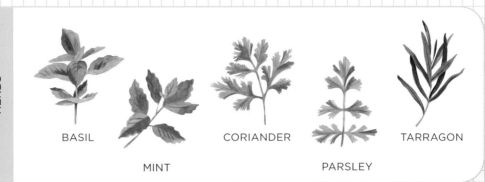

BASIL

MINT

CORIANDER

PARSLEY

TARRAGON

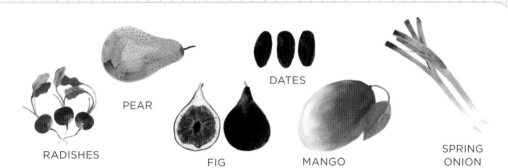

RADISHES

PEAR

DATES

FIG

MANGO

SPRING ONION

PUY LENTILS

CHICKPEAS

LEAVES

SPINACH

ROCKET

WATERCRESS

LAMB'S LETTUCE

RED ONION

BROWN ONION

SWEET POTATO

CHICORY

PARSNIP

CARROT

RED CABBAGE

POTATO

FENNEL

CAULIFLOWER

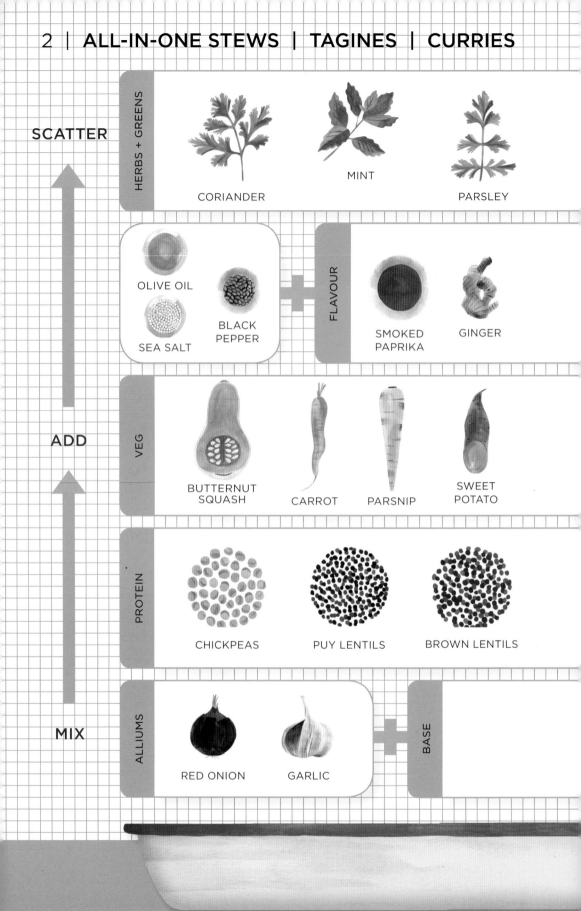

SCATTER

HERBS + GREENS

CORIANDER

MINT

PARSLEY

OLIVE OIL

SEA SALT

BLACK PEPPER

+

FLAVOUR

SMOKED PAPRIKA

GINGER

ADD

VEG

BUTTERNUT SQUASH

CARROT

PARSNIP

SWEET POTATO

PROTEIN

CHICKPEAS

PUY LENTILS

BROWN LENTILS

MIX

ALLIUMS

RED ONION

GARLIC

+

BASE

WATERCRESS

SPRING
ONION

SPINACH

ROCKET

CHILLI

CORIANDER
SEEDS

RAS EL HANOUT

CUMIN
SEEDS

KAFFIR LIME LEMONGRASS

CELERIAC

OKRA

FENNEL

BEETROOT

LEEK

CANNELLINI BEANS

KIDNEY BEANS

BLACK BEANS

BORLOTTI BEANS

COCONUT MILK

TINNED TOMATOES

VEGETABLE STOCK

DRESS

HERBS

BASIL

DILL

THYME

CHEESE

GOAT'S CHEESE

FETA

MOZZARELLA

OVEN

VEG – SLICED OR CUBED

BROCCOLI

CAULIFLOWER

BRUSSELS SPROUTS

CELERIAC

BUTTERNUT SQUASH

AUBERGINE

BEETROOT

LAYER

BASE

SEA SALT

BLACK PEPPER

PASTRY

ROSEMARY

OREGANO

PARSLEY

PARMESAN

GORGONZOLA
PICCANTE

CHEDDAR

FENNEL

MUSHROOM

POTATO

RED PEPPER

COURGETTE

ALLIUMS

RED ONION

BROWN
ONION

GARLIC

LEEK

SPRING
ONION

CRÈME
FRAÎCHE

YOGURT

DOUBLE CREAM

VEGETABLE STOCK

SCATTER

TEXTURE

ALMONDS   HAZELNUTS   PINE NUTS

HERBS

PARSLEY   CORIANDER   BASIL   MINT

ROAST

FLAVOUR

OLIVE OIL

BLACK PEPPER

SEA SALT

+

LEMON

LIME

SPRING ONION

VEG

BROCCOLI   ARTICHOKES IN OIL   MUSHROOM   TOMATO   SWEET POTATO

MIX

BASE GRAIN

PEARL BARLEY   SPELT   BULGUR WHEAT

PISTACHIOS

PEANUTS

WALNUTS

CASHEWS

THYME

ROSEMARY

SPINACH

WATERCRESS

ROCKET

GARLIC

HARISSA

CORIANDER
SEEDS

SUMAC

CHILLI

GINGER

RAS EL HANOUT

CUMIN SEEDS

BUTTERNUT
SQUASH

KALE

ASPARAGUS

BEETROOT

FENNEL

FARRO

BUCKWHEAT

BROWN RICE

ORZO

VEGETARIAN

VEGETARIAN

4 | QUICK

UNDER THIRTY MINUTES
IN THE OVEN

VEGETARIAN | **QUICK**

THE MOST INDULGENT QUICK COOK QUICHE: BROCCOLI, GORGONZOLA, CHILLI & WALNUT

GREEN MACHINE: ROASTED GREENS WITH RAS EL HANOUT, BULGUR WHEAT & RICOTTA

CREOLE SPICED LEEK & MUSHROOM TART

CRISPY KALE & BULGUR WHEAT SALAD WITH POMEGRANATES, PRESERVED LEMON, GOAT'S CHEESE & ALMONDS

COURGETTE, ASPARAGUS & GOAT'S CHEESE TART

SPICY HARISSA SPROUTS & BROCCOLI WITH HALLOUMI, SPINACH & COUS COUS

BAKED EGGS WITH BEETROOT, CELERIAC, DILL & FETA

FAJITA SPICED MUSHROOMS & PEPPERS WITH STILTON & SOUR CREAM

SQUASH & GORGONZOLA TART WITH FIGS & PECANS

CRISPY GNOCCHI WITH ROASTED PEPPERS, CHILLI, ROSEMARY, & RICOTTA

STORECUPBOARD PASTA BAKE: CRISPY RED PEPPER & CANNELLINI BEANS WITH GORGONZOLA

QUICK CHEESE & ONION TART

QUICK ROASTED FENNEL & BULGUR WHEAT WITH MOZZARELLA, FIGS, POMEGRANATE & DILL

CRISP CAULIFLOWER STEAKS WITH HARISSA & GOAT'S CHEESE

THE MOST INDULGENT QUICK COOK QUICHE: BROCCOLI, GORGONZOLA, CHILLI & WALNUT

Puff pastry as a base for quiche? Yes please. I could eat this unashamedly indulgent dish every week – it's so quick to put together. Broccoli and gorgonzola complement each other beautifully, with a slight kick from the chilli. Serve with a crunchy green salad.

Serves: 4
Prep: 10 minutes
Cook: 30 minutes

320g ready-rolled puff
  pastry sheet
300g broccoli florets, halved
½ red onion, finely chopped
1 teaspoon chilli flakes
125g gorgonzola piccante
30g walnuts, chopped
100ml single cream
4 free-range eggs
1 lemon, zest only
1 teaspoon sea salt
1 clove of garlic, crushed

1. Preheat the oven to 180°C fan/200°C/ gas 6 and line a small deep roasting tin with baking paper. Now cover the base of the tin with the puff pastry – you want it to come up the sides and hold all the filling in.

2. Scatter the broccoli florets, red onion, chilli flakes, walnuts and gorgonzola evenly over the pastry.

3. Beat the cream, eggs, lemon zest, sea salt and garlic together, then pour over the broccoli and cheese. Transfer to the oven and bake for 30 minutes, after which the pastry should be cooked and the centre of the quiche just wobbly.

4. Leave to sit in the tin for 10 minutes to cool down, then serve warm or at room temperature.

    Note: You can use the baking paper that the pastry comes wrapped in to line the base of your roasting tin.

GREEN MACHINE: ROASTED GREENS WITH RAS EL HANOUT, BULGUR WHEAT & RICOTTA

This is a lovely all-in-one dish, really brought together by the creaminess of the ricotta at the end. If the supermarket has inexplicably run out of ricotta, substitute thick Greek yogurt. Ras el hanout can vary in heat, so if you know yours isn't very spicy, add another teaspoon.

Serves: 2
Prep: 10 minutes
Cook: 25 minutes

200g bulgur wheat, rinsed
400ml boiling vegetable stock
225g long-stem broccoli
180g green beans
270g spring greens, roughly
    chopped
2 teaspoons ras el hanout
1 tablespoon olive oil
2 cloves of garlic, crushed
1 teaspoon sea salt

DRESSING
1 lemon, zest and juice
2 tablespoons olive oil
1 teaspoon sea salt
Freshly ground black pepper

TO SERVE
25g mint, finely chopped
A handful of toasted almonds
4 heaped tablespoons ricotta
A good pinch of ras el hanout

1. Preheat the oven to 180°C fan/200°C/ gas 6.

2. Tip the bulgur wheat into a roasting tin and pour over the vegetable stock. Toss the broccoli, green beans and spring greens in a bowl with the ras el hanout, olive oil, garlic and sea salt, then spread them over the bulgur wheat in the tin. Transfer to the oven and cook, uncovered, for 25 minutes.

3. Mix together the lemon zest and juice, olive oil, sea salt and black pepper and set aside. Once the greens and bulgur wheat are cooked (the bulgur should be soft and the vegetables crisp), pour over the dressing, add the mint and mix well. Serve scattered with the toasted almonds and ricotta and a good pinch of ras el hanout.

CREOLE SPICED LEEK & MUSHROOM TART

I love the combination of cayenne pepper, paprika and lemon in this cream cheese tart base: it works perfectly with the leeks and mushrooms. Serve with some lightly dressed spinach on the side and you've got a flavourful, filling dinner.

Serves: 4
Prep: 10 minutes
Cook: 30 minutes

1 x 320g ready-rolled puff
   pastry sheet
180g cream cheese
1 teaspoon smoked paprika
½ teaspoon cayenne pepper
1 lemon, zest and juice
Freshly ground black pepper
1½ teaspoons sea salt
100g mushrooms, thinly sliced
1 tablespoon olive oil
175g baby leeks, halved
   lengthways

TO SERVE
Spinach leaves

1. Preheat the oven to 180°C fan/200°C/ gas 6. Lay the pastry on a lined roasting tray and cut it down so that it is a couple of centimetres larger at each end than the leeks (see photograph).

2. Mix together the cream cheese, paprika, cayenne, lemon zest and juice, black pepper and ½ teaspoon of sea salt, then spread over the pastry, leaving a 2.5cm border around the edges.

3. Mix the mushrooms with half the oil and another ½ teaspoon of salt and scatter over the cream cheese. Mix the leeks with the remaining oil and another ½ teaspoon of salt, and lay them over the mushrooms. Transfer to the oven and cook for 30 minutes.

4. Serve the tart hot, with a green salad alongside.

CRISPY KALE & BULGUR WHEAT SALAD WITH POMEGRANATES, PRESERVED LEMON, GOAT'S CHEESE & ALMONDS

This quick, flavoursome bulgur wheat salad, infused with preserved lemon and ginger, is as good for dinner as it is for a lunchbox. Thanks are owed to Rowan, this book's editor, for the idea – I'd happily eat this every week.

Serves: 2
Prep: 10 minutes
Cook: 15 minutes

200g bulgur wheat, rinsed
5cm ginger, finely grated
2 preserved lemons, rind roughly chopped
1 teaspoon sea salt
400ml boiling water
200g kale or spring greens
½ tablespoon olive oil
1 heaped tablespoon za'atar
1 tablespoon lemon juice
1 tablespoon extra virgin olive oil
100g goat's cheese, crumbled
50g toasted whole almonds
1 pomegranate, seeds only
15g fresh coriander, roughly chopped

TO SERVE
Greek or natural yogurt

1. Preheat the oven to 200°C fan/220°C/ gas 7.

2. Mix the rinsed bulgur wheat with the ginger, preserved lemon, sea salt and boiling water in a roasting tin. Toss the kale or spring greens with the olive oil, then tip evenly over the bulgur wheat. Transfer to the oven and roast for 15 minutes.

3. Meanwhile, whisk together the za'atar, lemon juice and extra virgin olive oil to make a dressing, and set aside.

4. Mix the cooked bulgur and crispy kale with the dressing, then scatter over the goat's cheese, almonds, pomegranate seeds and coriander. Serve hot, with the yogurt alongside.

Note: Za'atar is a mix of sesame seeds, sumac, dried herbs and spices. It's readily available in supermarkets, but if you can get hold of some from a Palestinian or Israeli grocer, it'll be much fresher.

COURGETTE, ASPARAGUS & GOAT'S CHEESE TART

A simple weeknight dinner – I'm fairly sure a version of this grew out of a quick fridge raid before catching up on everyone's favourite Westerosi soap opera, but it turned out so well that it deserved more than one repeat. By all means substitute feta cheese for the goat's – it's lovely either way. Serve with simply dressed or roasted cherry tomatoes on the side.

Serves: 4
Prep: 10 minutes
Cook: 30 minutes

2 courgettes, very thinly sliced
    into rounds
200g asparagus
½ tablespoon olive oil
½ teaspoon sea salt
1 lemon, zest only
Freshly ground black pepper
A handful of fresh dill, roughly
    chopped
1 x 320g ready-rolled puff
    pastry sheet
2 tablespoons crème fraîche
100g goat's cheese with rind,
    thinly sliced

TO SERVE
Roasted or dressed cherry
    tomatoes

1. Preheat the oven to 180°C fan/200°C/ gas 6. Mix the courgettes and asparagus in a bowl with the oil, salt, lemon zest, black pepper and dill.

2. Lay the puff pastry on a lined roasting tray and spread with the crème fraîche, leaving a 2.5cm border around the edges. Arrange the courgette slices like fish scales, slightly overlapping, on top of the crème fraîche, then lay over first the goat's cheese slices, then the asparagus.

3. Transfer to the oven and cook for 30 minutes. Serve hot, with a salad or tomatoes alongside.

SPICY HARISSA SPROUTS & BROCCOLI WITH HALLOUMI, SPINACH & COUS COUS

This is a quick and easy dinner – the halloumi works so well with the spices, sprouts and broccoli. Pile into flatbreads with yogurt and you've got a filling meal.

Serves: 4
Prep: 10 minutes
Cook: 25 minutes

1 head of broccoli,
  cut into florets
500g Brussels sprouts
250g halloumi, cut into cubes
2 tablespoons harissa
2 tablespoons olive oil
150g spinach, chopped
A pinch of sea salt
½ lemon, juice only

TO SERVE
Flatbreads
4 tablespoons yogurt

1. Preheat the oven to 180°C fan/200°C/ gas 6.

2. Mix the broccoli with the sprouts, halloumi, harissa and olive oil in a roasting tin, then transfer to the oven and roast for 25 minutes.

3. Stir through the chopped spinach and taste and season with sea salt and lemon juice as needed. Serve piled into flatbreads with the yogurt.

BAKED EGGS WITH BEETROOT, CELERIAC, DILL & FETA

I love baked eggs: they're the perfect weekend breakfast or late-night comfort food. These started out in ramekins, like oeufs en cocotte, before I decided they'd be happier freeform on a roasting tray. The flavours in this dish are incredible – try it and see.

Serves: 4
Prep: 10 minutes
Cook: 20 minutes

180g fresh beetroot, peeled and grated
180g celeriac, peeled and grated
Any beetroot tops, finely chopped
3 tablespoons chopped fresh dill
180g natural yogurt
1½ tablespoons lemon juice
180g feta cheese
Freshly ground black pepper
4 free-range eggs

TO SERVE
A pinch of sea salt
Fresh dill
4 slices toasted buttered sourdough

1. Preheat the oven to 160°C fan/180°C/gas 4.

2. Mix together the grated beetroot and celeriac, beetroot tops, dill, yogurt, lemon juice and feta, along with a good grind of black pepper. Line a large roasting tin with baking paper, then divide the mixture into four piles, well spaced apart, and flatten them with a spoon in the centre to form a cup.

3. Crack an egg into each beetroot cup, then transfer to the oven and bake for 15–20 minutes, until the eggs are done to your liking.

4. Season the eggs with a pinch of sea salt, scatter with fresh dill and serve with toasted buttered sourdough alongside.

Note: The photograph opposite shows the eggs before baking.

FAJITA SPICED MUSHROOMS & PEPPERS WITH STILTON & SOUR CREAM

I love fajitas and this version with mushrooms is a wonderful quick dinner. You'll need to use the grill tray that comes fitted as standard in your oven to get everything cooking evenly: have the tortillas and sour cream ready on the table, so you can serve this as soon as it comes out of the oven.

Serves: 2–3
Prep: 10 minutes
Cook: 10 minutes

300g portobello mushrooms, sliced
150g chestnut mushrooms, sliced
2 red peppers, thinly sliced
1 onion, thinly sliced
1 teaspoon chipotle chilli flakes
2 teaspoons ground cumin
2 teaspoons ground coriander
2 teaspoons sea salt
1 tablespoon olive oil
25g fresh coriander, chopped
100g stilton
150ml sour cream
Warm tortillas

1. Preheat the grill to max. Tip the mushrooms, peppers and onion on to a grill tray large enough to hold everything in one layer, and mix with the spices, salt and olive oil. Transfer to the grill for 5–10 minutes, until the peppers are charred and the mushrooms have softened.

2. Scatter over the coriander and stilton and serve with the sour cream in warm tortillas.

SQUASH & GORGONZOLA TART WITH FIGS & PECANS

Gorgonzola and figs work beautifully with squash for a lovely autumnal dish. The trick with this tart, as with many of the squash dishes in the book, is to dice the squash into tiny 1cm cubes, so it'll cook through beautifully in half an hour.

Makes: 6
Prep: 15 minutes
Cook: 30 minutes

400g squash, peeled and cut into 1cm cubes
½ tablespoon olive oil
1 teaspoon sea salt
1 x 320g ready-rolled puff pastry sheet
1 heaped tablespoon crème fraîche
200g gorgonzola piccante
5 figs, quartered
A handful of fresh basil leaves
1 tablespoon honey
45g chopped pecans

1. Preheat the oven to 180°C fan/200°C/gas 6. Mix the squash cubes with the olive oil and sea salt.

2. Lay the puff pastry on a lined baking tray, and cut into six squares. Spread each with the crème fraîche, leaving a 1cm border around the edge. Scatter evenly with the squash, then the gorgonzola, and top with a few fig quarters and a basil leaf, then drizzle over the honey.

3. Transfer to the oven and cook for 20 minutes, then remove and scatter over the pecans. Return to the oven for a further 10 minutes, until the pastry is golden brown and the squash is cooked through.

4. Serve hot, scattered with more basil.

CRISPY GNOCCHI WITH ROASTED PEPPERS, CHILLI, ROSEMARY & RICOTTA

The gnocchi with mozzarella and tomatoes from the first *Roasting Tin* book was so popular that I decided to revisit it, as there are never too many ways to eat crispy gnocchi. This version, with roasted red peppers and rosemary, is a lovely alternative. Use a very large and ideally metal roasting tin, for maximum crunch on the potatoes.

Serves: 2 generously
Prep: 15 minutes
Cook: 30 minutes

500g gnocchi
500g mixed red, yellow and
   baby peppers, roughly
   chopped
200g cherry tomatoes, halved
2 tablespoons olive oil
2 bay leaves
2 cloves of garlic
1 teaspoon chilli flakes
2 large sprigs of fresh rosemary
1 teaspoon sea salt
Freshly ground black pepper
4 tablespoons ricotta
A handful of freshly chopped
   parsley

1. Preheat the oven to 200°C fan/220°C/ gas 7. Tip the gnocchi into a large bowl, then pour a kettleful of boiling water over it and leave to stand for 2 minutes before draining well.

2. Tip the gnocchi into a roasting tin along with everything except the ricotta. Mix well – make sure you've used a tin big enough for everything to fit in one layer. Transfer to the oven and cook for 30 minutes, until the gnocchi is crisp and golden.

3. Taste and season with salt and pepper as needed, dollop on the ricotta and scatter with the parsley before serving hot.

STORECUPBOARD PASTA BAKE: CRISPY RED PEPPER & CANNELLINI BEANS WITH GORGONZOLA

This is a good quick storecupboard pasta bake. I often buy jars of ready roasted red peppers, then don't know what to do with them – this is a perfect way to use them up. You can use any cheese you have lying about – I like the contrast of blue cheese with this, but feta or goat's cheese would be just as good.

Serves: 2–3
Prep: 10 minutes
Cook: 15 minutes

300g vine tomatoes, quartered
200g macaroni/ditalini
2 tablespoons olive oil
25g fresh dill, roughly chopped
25g fresh flat-leaf parsley,
    roughly chopped
1 x 450g jar of roasted red
    peppers, drained
    and roughly chopped
160g pitted black olives,
    halved
1 x 400g tin of cannellini beans,
    drained and rinsed
3 spring onions, finely chopped
2 teaspoons smoked paprika
½ lemon, juice only
100g Gorgonzola piccante,
    roughly crumbled
1 teaspoon sea salt
Freshly ground black pepper
50g panko breadcrumbs

1. Preheat the grill to max. Tip the tomatoes into a small lasagne dish, transfer to the oven and grill for 5–10 minutes, until softened.

2. Meanwhile, bring a large pan of salted water to the boil and cook the macaroni or ditalini for 9–11 minutes, or according to the packet instructions, until just al dente.

3. Drain the pasta, then stir in the grilled tomatoes, olive oil, herbs, red peppers, black olives, cannellini beans, spring onions, smoked paprika, lemon juice, half the cheese, the sea salt and a good grind of black pepper. Taste and adjust the lemon juice, salt and olive oil as needed.

4. Return the mixture to the lasagne dish, and scatter over the remaining cheese and the breadcrumbs. Drizzle with a little olive oil, then return to the grill for 3–5 minutes, until crisp and golden brown. Serve hot. Leftovers are excellent in a lunchbox.

QUICK CHEESE & ONION TART

Shallots, rather than onions, form the base for this five-ingredient cheese and onion tart – they become wonderfully sweet after half an hour. Really good for a quick post-work dinner, along with a crunchy green salad.

Serves: 4
Prep: 10 minutes
Cook: 30 minutes

400g banana/echalion shallots, peeled
1 tablespoon Dijon mustard
1 x 320g ready-rolled puff pastry sheet
80g mature Cheddar, grated
A few sprigs of fresh thyme
Freshly ground black pepper

TO SERVE
Green salad

1. Preheat the oven to 180°C fan/200°C/gas 6. Cut each shallot into four slices lengthways.

2. Lay out the pastry on a roasting tray lined with baking paper, and spread with the Dijon mustard, leaving a 2.5cm border around the edge. Arrange the flat shallot slices over the top, then scatter over the Cheddar, thyme and black pepper.

3. Transfer to the oven for 30 minutes. Serve hot with a green salad alongside.

QUICK ROASTED FENNEL & BULGUR WHEAT WITH MOZZARELLA, FIGS, POMEGRANATE & DILL

This is a beautiful dish, and perfect for a lunchbox the next day too. Do as Alice Hart suggests and buy the shorter, fatter bulbs of fennel – they have a better flavour.

Serves: 4
Prep: 10 minutes
Cook: 20 minutes

300g fennel, thinly sliced
300g bulgur wheat
2 cloves of garlic, crushed
600ml boiling vegetable stock
2–3 figs, quartered
250g mozzarella, roughly torn
1 pomegranate, seeds only
20g fresh dill, roughly chopped

DRESSING
1 orange, zest plus 1 tablespoon
   juice
1 tablespoon orange juice
1 tablespoon extra virgin
   olive oil
4 spring onions, thinly sliced
1 teaspoon sea salt
Freshly ground black pepper

1. Preheat the oven to 200°C fan/220°C/ gas 7.

2. Mix the fennel, bulgur wheat, garlic and boiling vegetable stock in a roasting tin, then transfer to the oven and cook for 20 minutes.

3. Meanwhile, whisk the orange zest, juice, extra virgin olive oil, spring onions, sea salt and black pepper together. Pour this dressing over the cooked bulgur wheat and fennel and mix well. Taste and adjust the seasoning as needed.

4. Scatter with the fig quarters, mozzarella, pomegranate seeds and chopped dill, and serve hot.

Note: Take the mozzarella, figs and pomegranate out of the fridge an hour before you want them, to let them come up to room temperature.

CRISP CAULIFLOWER STEAKS WITH HARISSA & GOAT'S CHEESE

This is one of the most visually beautiful dishes in the book, and tastes as good as it looks. Serve with Greek yogurt and some cous cous on the side.

Serves: 4
Prep: 10 minutes
Cook: 25–30 minutes

1 very large cauliflower
1 red onion, quartered
1 tablespoon olive oil
1 teaspoon sea salt
4 teaspoons harissa
125g soft goat's cheese, crumbled
30g pine nuts, roughly chopped
20g panko breadcrumbs
2 tablespoons fresh flat-leaf parsley, chopped

TO SERVE
Cous cous (see page 16)
Greek yogurt

1. Preheat the oven to 180°C fan/200°C/ gas 6. Remove the greens from the cauliflower and pop them into the roasting tin along with the red onion. Mix with the olive oil and season with salt.

2. Slice the cauliflower from top to bottom into four thick steaks and lay these in the tin along with the greens and red onion. Rub each steak on both sides with ½ teaspoon of harissa. Season with sea salt, then press the goat's cheese onto each steak.

3. Mix the pine nuts, panko breadcrumbs and parsley with a pinch of sea salt, then scatter a quarter of this over each cauliflower steak, pressing down lightly.

4. Drizzle with olive oil, then transfer to the oven to roast for 25–30 minutes, until the tops are golden brown and the cauliflower is just cooked through. Serve the steaks with cous cous and Greek yogurt, with the crispy leaves and onions alongside.

VEGETARIAN

5 | **MEDIUM**

UP TO 45 MINUTES
IN THE OVEN

VEGETARIAN | MEDIUM

OVEN BAKED SHAKSHUKA:
ROASTED PEPPERS, TOMATOES
& CHILLI WITH EGGS

CARROT & TALEGGIO
TARTE TATIN

MEDITERRANEAN COURGETTES
ROASTED WITH OLIVES,
FETA & TOMATOES

WATERCRESS & PARSNIP
PANZANELLA WITH GORGONZOLA,
HONEY & RADISHES

LEEK & PUY LENTIL GRATIN
WITH A CRUNCHY FETA TOPPING

HONEY ROASTED ROOT
VEGETABLE SALAD WITH BLUE
CHEESE & SPINACH

WENSLEYDALE, PARSNIP &
CARROT TART WITH ROSEMARY

CANNELLINI BEAN FALAFEL
WITH POTATO WEDGES,
SPINACH & POMEGRANATE

HERBY ROASTED PEPPERS
STUFFED WITH ARTICHOKES,
OLIVES & FETA

STUFFED ROASTED FENNEL
& MUSHROOMS WITH GRUYERE

RED WINE MUSHROOM
CASSEROLE WITH A CHEESE
COBBLER TOPPING

CRISPY SPROUT & ARTICHOKE
GRATIN WITH LEMON
& BLUE CHEESE

CHIPOTLE ROASTED SWEETCORN
WITH SQUASH, BLACK BEANS,
FETA & LIME

OVEN BAKED SHAKSHUKA: ROASTED PEPPERS, TOMATOES & CHILLI WITH EGGS

I love shakshuka, but I don't love how long it takes to carefully fry large quantities of onions, peppers and tomatoes on the stove. Cue the oven version – roast all the vegetables first, and save yourself 20 minutes of stirring. This is a standard weekend breakfast at home.

Serves: 4
Prep: 15 minutes
Cook: 45 minutes

1 red onion, roughly chopped
2 red peppers, roughly chopped
2 yellow peppers, roughly chopped
300g vine tomatoes, quartered
2 red chillies, deseeded and roughly chopped
2 cloves of garlic, crushed
1 tablespoon olive oil
1 teaspoon sea salt
1 teaspoon ground cumin
1 teaspoon ground coriander
1½ teaspoons smoked paprika
1 x 400g tin of chopped tomatoes
4 free-range eggs
1 tablespoon za'atar (optional)
Freshly chopped coriander

TO SERVE
Buttered toast or pitta breads

1. Preheat the oven to 180°C fan/200°C/gas 6.

2. Mix the onion, peppers, tomatoes, chillies and garlic with the oil, salt and spices in a large roasting tin, then transfer to the oven and roast for 30 minutes.

3. Lower the temperature to 160°C fan/180°C/gas 4. Squash the cooked tomatoes down well with a wooden spoon, then add the tinned tomatoes and mix everything together. Make four indentations in the tomato mixture, crack an egg into each, then return to the oven for a further 10 minutes, or until the eggs are just cooked to your liking.

4. Scatter with the za'atar, if using, and the freshly chopped coriander. Serve with lots of hot buttered toast or pitta breads.

Note: The eggs will take more or less time depending on whether they're fridge cold.

CARROT & TALEGGIO TARTE TATIN

This is a lovely tart to make if you've impulse-bought some tiny, green-topped Peter Rabbit carrots at the supermarket and are wondering what to do with them; it looks even prettier if there are rainbow carrots on offer. You don't need much more than a green salad alongside this for an elegant weeknight dinner.

Serves: 4
Prep: 10 minutes
Cook: 30 minutes

1 x 320g ready-rolled puff
   pastry sheet
2 scant teaspoons mustard
200g taleggio, thinly sliced
250g baby carrots, halved
   lengthways
1 tablespoon olive oil
1 teaspoon sea salt
Freshly ground black pepper
A few sprigs of fresh thyme

TO SERVE
Green salad

1. Preheat the oven to 180°C fan/200°C/gas 6. Lay the pastry on a lined baking tray and spread with the mustard, leaving a 2.5cm border around the edges, then scatter over the taleggio.

2. Toss the halved carrots with the olive oil and salt, then arrange these over the cheese. Scatter over the thyme, then transfer to the oven and roast for 30 minutes.

3. Serve hot, with a green salad alongside.

MEDITERRANEAN COURGETTES ROASTED WITH OLIVES, FETA & TOMATOES

Courgettes can be unfairly maligned, but try this storecupboard dish and you'll have new green-veg converts in your house. A bowl of lemony cous cous on the side makes for a lovely light dinner.

Serves: 4
Prep: 10 minutes
Cook: 35 minutes

6 large courgettes, cut into
  1cm diagonal slices
200g feta cheese,
  roughly chopped
140g sunblush tomatoes
  in olive oil
120g black olives
40g panko breadcrumbs
Freshly ground black pepper

TO SERVE
Cous cous (see page 16)

1. Preheat the oven to 180°C fan/200°C/ gas 6.

2. Put the courgette slices into a very large roasting tin in a single layer, then cover thickly with the feta cheese. Tip the sun-blush tomatoes and olives over evenly, then scatter with the breadcrumbs and plenty of black pepper. Transfer to the oven and roast for 35 minutes.

3. Ten minutes before you're ready to eat, prepare the cous cous, stirring through some lemon juice if you wish.

4. Serve the roasted courgettes with the cous cous alongside.

Note: If you've used sunblush tomatoes in olive oil, you don't need to add any extra oil to the dish – there's enough on the tomatoes. If you're using dried tomatoes from a packet, mix a tablespoon of oil with the courgettes before adding the feta.

WATERCRESS & PARSNIP PANZANELLA WITH GORGONZOLA, HONEY & RADISHES

The tin opposite didn't last very long once the picture had been shot: everyone kept diving in to fish out bits of honey-drizzled parsnip and gorgonzola. A very moreish warm salad.

Serves: 2
Prep: 10 minutes
Cook: 30 minutes

2 bread rolls (ciabatta,
  sourdough, bagels),
  roughly torn
500g parsnips, peeled and
  cut into 1cm half-moons
1 tablespoon olive oil
1 clove of garlic, crushed
2–3 sprigs of fresh rosemary
1 teaspoon sea salt
120g watercress
100g radishes, thinly sliced
100g gorgonzola piccante
1 tablespoon runny honey

DRESSING
2 teaspoons red wine vinegar
2 teaspoons extra virgin
  olive oil
1 teaspoon sea salt
A good grind of black pepper

1. Preheat the oven to 180°C fan/200°C/gas 6.

2. Mix the torn bread, parsnips, olive oil, garlic, rosemary and sea salt in a roasting tin, then transfer to the oven and roast for 30 minutes.

3. Meanwhile, whisk together the red wine vinegar, extra virgin olive oil, sea salt and black pepper and set aside.

4. Mix the roast parsnips and toasted bread with the watercress, radishes, gorgonzola and dressing. Pile on to plates and drizzle over the honey just before serving.

LEEK & PUY LENTIL GRATIN
WITH A CRUNCHY FETA TOPPING

This filling gratin, with its crisp feta topping, is perfect comfort food – the dining equivalent of sitting cosily on the sofa under a blanket. It's good for batch cooking for the week ahead, as any leftovers will keep well for a couple of days in the fridge. This dish is a favourite among friends who helped try out the recipes.

Serves: 4 generously
Prep: 10 minutes
Cook: 40 minutes

30g butter
3 cloves of garlic, crushed
500g leeks, thinly sliced
2 teaspoons sea salt
Freshly ground black pepper
500g vac-packed cooked
  Puy lentils
450ml crème fraîche
125g feta cheese, crumbled
50g panko or fresh white
  breadcrumbs
1 tablespoon olive oil

1. Preheat the oven to 180°C fan/200°C/ gas 6. Put the butter and garlic into a roasting tin and pop into the oven to melt while you get on with slicing the leeks.

2. Mix the sliced leeks with the melted garlic butter, season well with the sea salt and black pepper, then return to the oven to roast for 20 minutes.

3. After 20 minutes, stir through the Puy lentils, crème fraîche and another good scatter of sea salt, then top with the feta cheese and breadcrumbs. Drizzle with the olive oil, then return to the oven for a further 20–25 minutes, until golden brown on top.

4. Serve the gratin hot, with a mustard or balsamic dressed green salad alongside.

HONEY ROASTED ROOT VEGETABLE SALAD: WITH BLUE CHEESE & SPINACH

This warming winter salad works well as a light main for two, or alongside a more substantial grain-based dish.

Serves: 4
Prep: 10 minutes
Cook: 45 minutes

400g carrots, peeled
  and cut into 5mm slices
400g parsnips, peeled
  and cut into 5mm slices
450g celeriac, peeled
  and cut into 5mm wedges
2 teaspoons paprika
2 tablespoons olive oil
5cm ginger, grated
2 teaspoons sea salt
1 tablespoon honey
45g walnuts, roughly broken
100g baby spinach leaves
100g blue cheese, e.g. Stilton

DRESSING
2 teaspoons red wine vinegar
1 tablespoon extra virgin
  olive oil
1 teaspoon sea salt
Freshly ground black pepper

1. Preheat the oven to 200°C fan/220°C/ gas 7.

2. Mix the carrots, parsnips and celeriac in a roasting tin along with the paprika, oil, ginger and salt, then transfer to the oven and roast for 40 minutes.

3. Drizzle everything with the honey, add the walnuts, then return to the oven for 5 minutes.

4. Meanwhile, whisk the red wine vinegar with the extra virgin olive oil, sea salt and black pepper.

5. Once the vegetables are done, give them 5 minutes to cool down, then tip the spinach and blue cheese into the roasting tin along with the dressing and mix well. Taste and adjust the salt or honey as needed and serve immediately.

WENSLEYDALE, PARSNIP & CARROT TART WITH ROSEMARY

I'm not going to deny it – this is a time-consuming dish, in the way that stuffing vine leaves or kibbeh is time-consuming, but worth it. If you feel like a bit of kitchen pottering, then this is the dish for you: there's something curiously soothing about repetitive ribbon rolling. It tastes as good as it looks.

Serves: 4
Prep: 30 minutes
Cook: 40 minutes

1 x 320g ready-rolled puff
   pastry sheet
2 tablespoons crème fraîche
200g Wensleydale cheese,
   finely crumbled
2–3 large carrots, peeled
2–3 large parsnips, peeled
1 tablespoon olive oil
2 teaspoons sea salt
Freshly ground black pepper
A few sprigs of fresh rosemary
2 cloves of garlic

TO SERVE
Green salad

1. Preheat the oven to 180°C/200°C/gas 6. Unroll the puff pastry on to a large roasting tray, then spread with the crème fraîche, leaving a 2.5cm border around the edge. Scatter over the crumbled cheese.

2. Using a speed peeler, peel the carrots and parsnips into long ribbons and transfer them to a large bowl. Dress with the olive oil, sea salt and black pepper, then roll each ribbon into a small cylinder. Prod each cylinder into the Wensleydale as you go, roughly alternating the white and orange, until the cheese is completely covered in parsnip and carrot roses.

3. Congratulate yourself on a job well done, then scatter the tart with a little rosemary, transfer to the oven and roast for 40 minutes. Serve hot, with a green salad alongside.

CANNELLINI BEAN FALAFEL WITH POTATO WEDGES, SPINACH & POMEGRANATE

A little bit of effort is required before sticking these in the roasting tin, but it's worth it. They are lovely for a light, snacky dinner or as a starter.

Serves: 2–3
Prep: 10 minutes
Cook: 40 minutes

1 x 400g tin of cannellini beans
½ clove of garlic, crushed
50g chives, finely chopped
200g feta cheese, crumbled
2 teaspoons smoked paprika
2 sweet potatoes, peeled and
   cut into small wedges
1 tablespoon olive oil
½ teaspoon sea salt

TO SERVE
150g baby spinach leaves
1 pomegranate, seeds only
4 tablespoons natural yogurt

1. Preheat the oven to 180°C fan/200°C/ gas 6. Pulse the cannellini beans, garlic, chives, feta and smoked paprika together in a food processor until you have a rough, sticky mixture.

2. Tip the sweet potato wedges into a large roasting tin and mix with the olive oil and sea salt. Take walnut-size portions of the falafel mix and roll them into balls, then tuck them around the sweet potato wedges.

3. Transfer to the oven and roast for 40 minutes, until the sweet potatoes are cooked through, and the falafel are golden brown on top.

4. Serve with the spinach, pomegranate seeds and natural yogurt alongside.

   Note: The falafel mix doesn't get sufficiently sticky if you try to hand mix it, so do use a food processor.

HERBY ROASTED PEPPERS STUFFED WITH ARTICHOKES, OLIVES & FETA

Stuffed peppers – retro or fantastic? As with pineapple upside-down cake, I think they are both. These lovely parcels, stuffed with rich artichokes and feta, are a far cry from the ones that turned up in school dinners, and show just how lovely stuffed vegetables can be.

Serves: 4
Prep: 10 minutes
Cook: 35 minutes

4 long red peppers, halved
    lenthways and deseeded
1 x 280g jar of artichokes,
    roughly chopped
200g feta cheese, crumbled
100g pine nuts
Freshly ground black pepper
25g fresh flat-leaf parsley, finely
    chopped
1 lemon, zest and juice
50g breadcrumbs
1 tablespoon olive oil

TO SERVE
Focaccia or good bread
Crunchy green salad

1. Preheat the oven to 200°C fan/220°C/ gas 7. Arrange the halved peppers in a lined roasting tin with plenty of room around them.

2. Mix the artichokes, feta cheese, pine nuts, black pepper, parsley, lemon zest and juice and half the breadcrumbs, and stuff the mixture into the halved peppers.

3. Top with the remaining breadcrumbs, drizzle over the olive oil, then transfer to the oven to roast for 30–35 minutes, until the peppers are softened and slightly charred around the edges and the topping is crisp and golden.

4. Serve hot, with a crunchy green salad and good bread alongside.

STUFFED ROASTED FENNEL & MUSHROOMS WITH GRUYERE

Fennel is a divisive issue in my kitchen – I like it, my boyfriend doesn't: he has been known to pick all the fennel out of dishes that I've asked him to try from this book. So this dish has hidden fennel in the mushrooms, and obvious fennel for the rest of us.

Serves: 2
Prep: 15 minutes
Cook: 40 minutes

2 plump fennel bulbs, halved
150g chestnut mushrooms, finely chopped
75g Gruyère cheese, grated
15g fresh tarragon, finely chopped
1 lemon, zest only
1 teaspoon sea salt
Freshly ground black pepper
4 portobello mushrooms, stems removed
40g white breadcrumbs
1 tablespoon olive oil

1. Preheat the oven to 180°C fan/200°C/gas 6. Carefully cut out the centre of each fennel bulb, leaving a 'shell' behind. Chop the remaining flesh, and mix it with the chopped mushrooms, Gruyère, tarragon, lemon zest, salt and pepper.

2. Stuff this mixture into the fennel shells and the mushroom cups, then cover each with the breadcrumbs. Drizzle with olive oil, then transfer to the oven and roast for 40 minutes, until the tops are golden brown and crisp.

3. Serve with a salad and crusty bread alongside.

RED WINE MUSHROOM CASSEROLE WITH A CHEESE COBBLER TOPPING

This casserole is incredibly warming for a cold autumn night – rich with wine and mushrooms and with herby cheese scones as a topping. You can easily double this up to serve more people – just use a really large roasting tin.

Serves: 2
Prep: 10 minutes
Cook: 40 minutes

300g mini portobello mushrooms
250g chestnut mushrooms, halved
3 cloves of garlic, crushed
2 teaspoons sea salt
1 onion, roughly chopped
2-3 sprigs of fresh rosemary
1 tablespoon olive oil
200ml good red wine
2 teaspoons cornflour
150ml vegetable stock

SCONES
250g plain flour
1½ teaspoons cream of tartar
1 teaspoon sea salt
35g cold butter, cubed
25g fresh parsley or basil, finely chopped
60g extra mature cheddar, grated
Freshly ground black pepper
100ml milk
1 egg, lightly beaten

1. Preheat the oven to 180°C fan/200°C/ gas 6. Mix the mushrooms, garlic, sea salt, onion and rosemary with the olive oil in a roasting tin or lasagne dish, then transfer to the oven and roast for 20 minutes.

2. Meanwhile, in a food processor or by hand, mix the flour, cream of tartar and sea salt with the butter until it looks like fine sand, then stir in the herbs, three-quarters of the cheese and the pepper. Add the milk, and bring everything together gently into a scone dough. Cover and chill until needed.

3. Once the mushrooms have had their 20 minutes, mix a tablespoon of the red wine with the cornflour then stir it into the mushrooms along with the remaining wine and the stock.

4. Form the scone dough into walnut-size portions and dot them over the mushrooms, flattening each slightly. Brush with the beaten egg, top with the reserved cheese, then return to the oven for 20 minutes – the scones should be golden brown and crisp, and the sauce thick and reduced. Leave to sit for 5 minutes, then serve hot.

CRISPY SPROUT & ARTICHOKE GRATIN WITH LEMON & BLUE CHEESE

Not everyone shares my love for sprouts, but this might convert the most hardened sceptic. Rich artichoke is a lovely pairing in this rich, crisp gratin – perfect for a cold night.

Serves: 4
Prep: 10 minutes
Cook: 25 minutes

400g Brussels sprouts, halved
175g jarred artichokes, roughly chopped
1 tablespoon oil from the jarred artichokes
300ml single cream
1 tablespoon lemon juice
100g stilton, crumbled
A good grind of black pepper
50g panko breadcrumbs

1. Preheat the oven to 180°C fan/200°C/ gas 6.

2. Mix the sprouts, artichokes, oil, single cream and lemon juice together in a roasting tin, then top with the crumbled stilton, black pepper and panko bread-crumbs. Transfer to the oven and roast for 25–30 minutes, until the top is golden brown and bubbling.

3. Serve hot, with thinly sliced toasted sourdough alongside.

CHIPOTLE ROASTED SWEETCORN WITH SQUASH, BLACK BEANS, FETA & LIME

This dish feels like a festival to me, with its bright colours and textures – crispy black beans, soft feta, spiced squash and toasted corn on the cob. Serve as part of a Mexican style sharing feast, or on its own with coriander rice.

Serves: 4
Prep: 10 minutes
Cook: 45 minutes

750g squash, cut into 1cm slices
4 sweetcorn
1 x 400g tin of black beans,
   drained and rinsed
1 teaspoon chipotle chilli flakes
1 teaspoon ground coriander
1 teaspoon ground cumin
1 teaspoon salt
2 tablespoons olive oil
1 lime, juice only
200g feta cheese, crumbled
25g fresh coriander,
   finely chopped
2 spring onions, finely chopped

TO SERVE
4 heaped tablespoons sour
   cream
Coriander rice
   (see page 17)

1. Preheat the oven to 180°C fan/200°C/ gas 6.

2. Mix together the squash, sweetcorn and black beans in a roasting tin along with the spices, salt and olive oil, then transfer to the oven and roast for 45 minutes.

3. Squeeze over the lime juice, then scatter over the feta, coriander and spring onions. Serve with the sour cream and rice alongside.

VEGETARIAN

6 | SLOW

AN HOUR +
IN THE OVEN

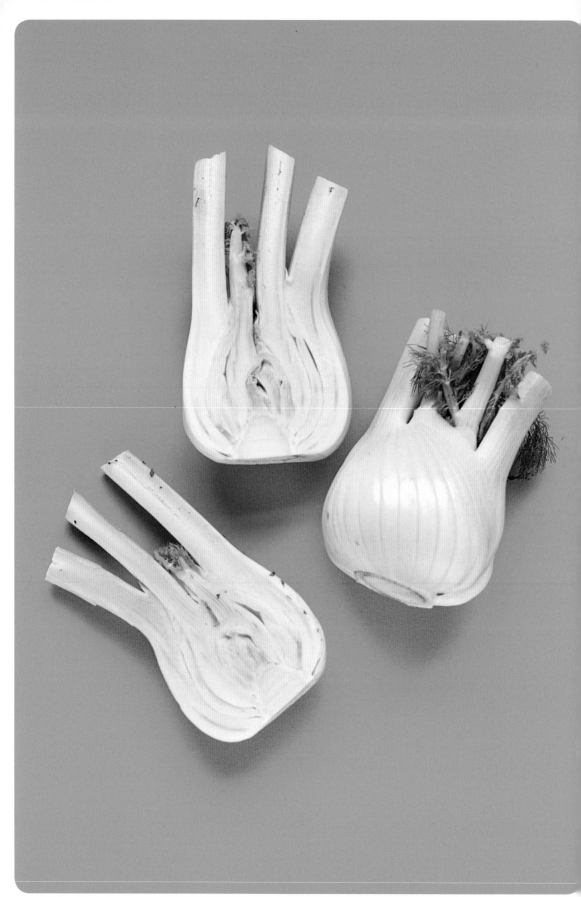

VEGETARIAN
SLOW

WHOLE STUFFED MINI PUMPKINS
WITH SAGE & GOAT'S CHEESE

AUBERGINE & FENNEL GRATIN
WITH GOAT'S CHEESE & WALNUTS

HASSELBACK SQUASH
WITH ROASTED ONIONS,
LEEKS & FETA

ALL-IN-ONE JEWELLED PEARL
BARLEY WITH SQUASH,
POMEGRANATE, WATERCRESS
& FETA

BASIL & THYME ROASTED ONIONS
WITH SQUASH, GOAT'S CHEESE
& WALNUTS

RICH POTATO & MUSHROOM
GRATIN WITH CREAM
& REBLOCHON

SWEET POTATOES WITH
TALEGGIO, ONIONS & BASIL

HERB STUFFED ROASTED ONIONS
WITH CHERRY TOMATOES
& CANNELLINI BEANS

LUX WARM WINTER SALAD:
ROASTED POTATOES & CELERIAC
WITH TRUFFLE, PARMESAN
& SOFT-BOILED EGGS

BUTTER ROASTED HARISSA
LEEKS & BEETROOT WITH
BULGUR WHEAT & FETA

CRUNCHY ROAST POTATO,
ARTICHOKE & SPRING GREEN
HASH WITH BAKED EGGS

WHOLE STUFFED MINI PUMPKINS WITH SAGE & GOAT'S CHEESE

These beautiful little pumpkins are a real showstopper. You can find them in supermarkets around Hallowe'en, or alternatively use very small squash. They can be very be very hard to cut so you will need a sharp, strong knife.

Serves: 4
Prep: 10 minutes
Cook: 1 hour

4 mini pumpkins
Sea salt
16 fresh sage leaves
250g soft goat's cheese
2 teaspoons chilli flakes
2½ tablespoons olive oil
½ teaspoon chilli powder

1. Preheat the oven to 180°C fan/200°C/ gas 6. Carefully slice the top off each pumpkin, then using a small sharp knife, cut around the cavity containing the seeds. Scoop these out with a spoon and set aside.

2. Season the inside of each cavity with a good pinch of sea salt, then line with two sage leaves. Stuff each with a quarter of the goat's cheese, then scatter over the chilli flakes before replacing the lid. Rub each pumpkin with ½ tablespoon of the olive oil, scatter with a little more salt, and top each pumpkin with more sage leaves, making sure there's plenty of oil on the leaves too. Transfer to the oven and roast for 1 hour.

3. Rub the pumpkin seeds with kitchen paper to get rid of any flesh and toss with ½ tablespoon of olive oil, the chilli powder and a pinch of sea salt. Ten minutes before the pumpkins are ready, tip the seeds into the roasting tin alongside, then return to the oven.

4. Serve the pumpkins whole, along with a green salad.

AUBERGINE & FENNEL GRATIN
WITH GOAT'S CHEESE & WALNUTS

Aubergine is often paired with a tomato sauce in a gratin, but it works beautifully with crème fraîche, goat's cheese and nutmeg in this warming layered fennel dish. The walnuts add extra crunch and flavour to the golden breadcrumb topping.

Serves: 4
Prep: 15 minutes
Cook: 45 minutes

600ml crème fraîche
2 teaspoons sea salt
Freshly ground black pepper
25g fresh flat-leaf parsley,
   finely chopped
1 teaspoon grated nutmeg
2 medium aubergines, thinly
   sliced into rounds
500g fennel, thinly sliced
125g soft goat's cheese,
   crumbled
50g white breadcrumbs
50g walnuts, roughly chopped
1 tablespoon olive oil

TO SERVE
Crusty bread

1. Preheat the oven to 180°C fan/200°C/ gas 6. Mix the crème fraîche with the sea salt, black pepper, parsley and nutmeg.

2. Place half of the aubergine slices into the tin, followed by half the fennel and half the crème fraîche and goat's cheese. Repeat these layers, then scatter the top layer of crème fraîche and cheese with the breadcrumbs and walnuts.

3. Drizzle with the olive oil, then transfer to the oven and bake for 45 minutes, until the top is golden brown and crisp, and the gratin is bubbling.

4. Leave to sit for 10 minutes to cool down before serving with plenty of crusty bread

Note: To get the fennel sliced really thinly, you can carefully use a mandolin or the slicing blade on a food processor.

HASSELBACK SQUASH WITH ROASTED ONIONS, LEEKS & FETA

Hasselback squash seems to be in vogue at the moment: think Hasselback potatoes, but bigger – they make a good-looking centrepiece. This dish incorporates leeks, which soften and squash down into a lovely rich gravy.

Serves: 4
Prep: 15 minutes
Cook: 1 hour 10 minutes

1 medium butternut squash
A handful of fresh rosemary
A handful of fresh thyme
6 bay leaves
2 red onions, halved crossways
2 leeks, cut into 2.5cm logs
50g butter, thinly sliced
1 teaspoon sea salt
300ml vegetable stock
4 tablespoons crème fraîche
100g feta cheese, crumbled

1. Preheat the oven to 180°C fan/200°C/gas 6. Carefully halve the squash, remove the seeds, then place cut side down on a board. Cut almost all the way through the squash, but not quite – you want a series of parallel cuts, as if making a hedgehog.

2. Stuff each cut alternately with rosemary, thyme and bay, then transfer to a roasting tin along with the onions and leeks. Lay the sliced butter over the squash and onions, and season with the sea salt. Pour the stock into the tin, then transfer to the oven and roast for 1 hour 10 minutes.

3. Prod the softened leeks with a wooden spoon and stir through the crème fraîche. Scatter the crumbled feta over the squash, and serve alongside the onion and leek gravy.

ALL-IN-ONE JEWELLED PEARL BARLEY WITH SQUASH, POMEGRANATE, WATERCRESS & FETA

This is a vibrant, elegant dinner: the pearl barley cooks beautifully in the oven along with the squash, with the fresh elements added just at the end. Excellent for lunchboxes the next day, too.

Serves: 4
Prep: 15 minutes
Cook: 1 hour

1 x 750g squash, peeled and cut
   into 1cm chunks
All the seeds from the squash
   (or a handful of pumpkin
   seeds if that's easier)
Sea salt
1 teaspoon olive oil
300g pearl barley, rinsed
700ml boiling vegetable stock
2 cloves of garlic, crushed
1 bag of watercress, roughly
   chopped
1 tablespoon lime juice
1 tablespoon extra virgin
   olive oil
100g feta cheese, crumbled
1 pomegranate, seeds only
Freshly ground black pepper

1. Preheat the oven to 200°C fan/220°C/ gas 7. Tip the squash chunks into the roasting tin, then spread the seeds you've saved from the squash on another baking tray and rub with a pinch of sea salt and the olive oil.

2. Mix the pearl barley, vegetable stock and crushed garlic with the squash chunks, then cover tightly with foil and transfer to the oven to cook for 1 hour. Pop the tray with the seeds in alongside after 50 minutes.

3. Once the squash and pearl barley have had an hour, remove from the oven and stir through the watercress, lime juice and extra virgin olive oil.

4. Top with the feta, pomegranate seeds and toasted seeds. Season with sea salt and black pepper to taste and serve hot.

BASIL & THYME ROASTED ONIONS WITH SQUASH, GOAT'S CHEESE & WALNUTS

This is such a lovely autumnal dish and looks beautiful when brought to the table: it's the favourite of this book's designer, Pene. Serve with a green salad and good bread.

Serves: 4
Prep: 10 minutes
Cook: 50 minutes

600g butternut squash, peeled and cut into 1cm chunks
4 medium onions, halved
1 tablespoon olive oil
1 teaspoon sea salt
Freshly ground black pepper
4 cloves of garlic, unpeeled and halved
8 fresh basil leaves
A handful of fresh thyme sprigs
125g soft goat's cheese (without rind)
A handful of roughly broken toasted walnuts

DRESSING
30g fresh basil, very finely chopped
3 tablespoons olive oil
1 teaspoon sea salt
½ tablespoon lemon juice

Note: If your onions are large, give them 50 minutes in the oven before topping with the goat's cheese.

1. Preheat the oven to 200°C fan/220°C/ gas 7. Arrange the squash and onions in a single layer in a roasting tin or large lasagne dish, the onions cut side up. Mix everything well with the olive oil, then scatter over the salt and black pepper.

2. Top each halved onion with half a clove of garlic, a basil leaf and a sprig of thyme and scatter the remaining thyme over the squash. Transfer to the oven and roast for 40 minutes.

3. Remove the dish from the oven and roughly break the goat's cheese over the onions and squash in large chunks, making sure each onion gets a piece of cheese over it. Scatter over the walnuts, then return to the oven for a further 10 minutes, until the onions are soft through when pierced with a fork.

4. Meanwhile, mix the chopped basil, olive oil, sea salt and lemon juice together. Once the onions are ready, pour over the dressing, and serve hot.

RICH POTATO & MUSHROOM GRATIN WITH CREAM & REBLOCHON

Somewhere between a tartiflette and a dauphinoise, this rich gratin takes elements from both and combines them for a very satisfying, if calorific, winter dish. (I have been known to have leftovers for breakfast.) If you can't find a reblochon, substitute Gruyère and layer it in between the gratin as well. Serve with a green salad.

Serves: 6
Prep: 15 minutes
Cook: 1 hour

1kg Maris Piper potatoes,
  sliced paper thin
1 onion, finely sliced
300g chestnut mushrooms,
  thinly sliced
Sea salt
Freshly ground black pepper
Fresh nutmeg
2 cloves of garlic, grated
800ml double cream
1 x 240g reblochon cheese
10–12 fresh sage leaves

TO SERVE
Green salad

1. Preheat the oven to 180°C fan/200°C/ gas 6. Butter a medium-sized roasting tin or lasagne dish, then add a layer of potatoes, followed by onions and mushrooms. Season with a generous pinch of sea salt, black pepper and a grating of nutmeg, then repeat the layers, seasoning between each, finishing with a layer of potatoes.

2. Mix the garlic with the double cream, another good pinch of salt, pepper and grated nutmeg, then pour it all over the potatoes. Top with the reblochon, scatter over the sage leaves, then transfer to the oven and cook for 1 hour.

3. Let the gratin sit for 10 minutes, then serve with a crisp green salad alongside.

   Note: It might seem like you're adding a lot of salt, but the potatoes absolutely drink it in: you may need to serve salt on the table so people can season to taste.

SWEET POTATO WITH TALEGGIO, ONIONS & BASIL

Whole roasted sweet potato was a university staple, given a new lease of life by my friend Laura. She perfected softening finely chopped red onions and garlic together to pile into the hot potatoes, along with a good dollop of Greek yogurt. This version, with rich taleggio and a basil dressing, is perfect comfort food.

Serves: 4
Prep: 15 minutes
Cook: 1 hour

4 sweet potatoes (about 1kg)
2 red onions, quartered
1 tablespoon olive oil
1 teaspoon sea salt
A handful of lemon thyme
  sprigs
200g taleggio, thickly sliced

DRESSING
30g fresh basil, very finely
  chopped
3 tablespoons olive oil
1 clove of garlic, finely grated
1 teaspoon sea salt
½ tablespoon lemon juice

1. Preheat the oven to 180°C fan/200°C/ gas 6.

2. Prick the sweet potatoes all over with a fork, then tip them into a roasting tin with the quartered onions. Rub the potatoes and onions with the oil and salt, then scatter over the lemon thyme. Transfer to the oven and roast for 55 minutes.

3. For the dressing, mix the chopped basil with the olive oil, garlic, sea salt and lemon juice and set aside.

4. When the sweet potatoes have had 55 minutes, take the tray out of the oven and cut a cross into each potato – they should be wonderfully soft inside. Lay the slices of taleggio inside the potatoes, then return to the oven for a further 5 minutes for the cheese to melt. Serve hot, with the onions and dressing alongside.

HERB STUFFED ROASTED ONIONS WITH CHERRY TOMATOES & CANNELLINI BEANS

In this dish, the onions are stuffed with butter and herbs and roasted whole. They make a lovely simple dinner along with the easy tomato and cannellini bean stew.

Serves: 4
Prep: 10 minutes
Cook: 1 hour

4 red onions
A handful of fresh thyme sprigs
A handful of fresh rosemary
  sprigs
75g butter
1 x 400g tin of cannellini beans,
  drained and rinsed
250g cherry tomatoes
200ml vegetable stock
2 bay leaves
Sea salt
Freshly ground black pepper
½ lemon, juice only
100g feta cheese, crumbled
A handful of fresh flat-leaf
  parsley, roughly chopped

1. Preheat the oven to 180°C fan/200°C/gas 6. Cut a tiny section off the base of each onion, so that it sits upright, then cut a deep cross in it, making sure not to cut all the way through. Transfer to a roasting tin, and stuff each one with a few sprigs of rosemary and thyme and a quarter of the butter.

2. Tip the cannellini beans, tomatoes and stock into the tin alongside the onions and add the remaining herbs and the bay leaves. Season the onions and tomatoes well with sea salt and black pepper, then transfer to the oven and roast for 1 hour.

3. Once cooked through, season the cannellini beans with the lemon juice and salt to taste. Scatter over the crumbled feta and parsley and serve hot.

LUX WARM WINTER SALAD:
ROASTED POTATOES & CELERIAC WITH
TRUFFLE, PARMESAN & SOFT-BOILED EGGS

This is such a rich dish – parmesan, egg and truffle were made to go with roast potatoes. The celeriac adds freshness, and there's pepper from the watercress – perfect. You can easily cook the eggs in the tin for the last 10 minutes, as with the roast potato hash on page 218, but I prefer the look and texture of soft-boiled eggs with this.

Serves: 4
Prep: 10 minutes
Cook: 45 minutes

500g Maris Piper potatoes,
   peeled and cut into 2.5cm
   chunks
500g celeriac, peeled and cut
   into 2.5cm chunks
3 cloves of garlic
1 tablespoon olive oil
1 teaspoon sea salt
Freshly ground black pepper
4 free-range eggs,
   at room temperature
100g watercress, roughly
   chopped
50g walnuts, toasted
25g parmesan, shaved

DRESSING
2 tablespoons olive oil
½ tablespoon lemon juice
1 teaspoon good-quality
   truffle oil
1 teaspoon sea salt
Freshly ground black pepper

1. Preheat the oven to 180°C fan/200°C/ gas 6. Tip the potatoes, celeriac and garlic into a roasting tin and mix well with the olive oil, sea salt and black pepper. Transfer to the oven and roast for 45 minutes, until the potatoes are crisp and cooked through.

2. Mix all the dressing ingredients together. Truffle oil comes in varying strengths, so you may wish to add a little more along with the lemon juice, a drop at a time, until you're happy with the taste.

3. Just before the potatoes are ready, bring a pan of water to the boil, then gently lower in the eggs and cook for 4–5 minutes for a runny yolk. Remove to a bowl of cold water and peel when cool enough to handle.

4. Mix the potatoes with the chopped watercress and top with the halved boiled eggs. Drizzle the dressing over everything, scatter over the walnuts and parmesan and serve hot.

BUTTER ROASTED HARISSA LEEKS & BEETROOT WITH BULGUR WHEAT & FETA

This tasty all-in-one dish is as good for dinner as it is for lunchboxes the next day. Harissa paste does tend to vary in strength, so try a tiny bit before you start to assess the level of heat, and put a bit more or less in the recipe as you prefer.

Serves: 2 generously
Prep: 10 minutes
Cook: 1 hour

350g beetroot, diced
  into 1cm chunks
2 leeks (450g), cut into
  2.5cm logs
1–2 tablespoons rose harissa
1 tablespoon softened butter
1 teaspoon sea salt
200g bulgur wheat
400ml boiling vegetable stock
100g feta cheese
A handful of fresh coriander,
  roughly chopped
4 tablespoons natural yogurt

1. Preheat the oven to 180°C fan/200°C/ gas 6.

2. Rub the beetroot and leeks all over with the harissa and butter in a roasting tin. Scatter over the salt, then transfer to the oven and roast for 45 minutes.

3. Give the vegetables a good mix, then stir in the bulgur wheat and vegetable stock. Return to the oven for 15 minutes, uncovered.

4. Scatter over the feta cheese and coriander and serve hot, with the yogurt on the side.

CRUNCHY ROAST POTATO, ARTICHOKE & SPRING GREEN HASH WITH BAKED EGGS

This is as good for a weekend breakfast as it is for a warming dinner: all your food groups in one gloriously crisp, eggy hash. The chilli yogurt brings everything together and you could scatter it with chopped coriander or any other soft herbs to finish if you wish.

Serves: 4
Prep: 10 minutes
Cook: 1 hour

800g floury potatoes (e.g. Maris Piper), peeled and cut into 2.5cm chunks
2 x 280g jars of sliced artichokes, drained
2 tablespoons oil from the artichokes
2 cloves of garlic, crushed
2 teaspoons sea salt
A good grind of black pepper
200g spring greens, roughly sliced
4 free-range eggs
½ tablespoon sriracha or your favourite hot chilli sauce
3 tablespoons natural yogurt

1. Preheat the oven to 200°C fan/220°C/ gas 7.

2. Mix the potatoes, artichokes, oil, garlic, salt and black pepper in a roasting tin, then transfer to the oven and roast for 50 minutes.

3. Reduce the heat to 150°C fan/170°C/ gas 4, and remove the tin from the oven. Stir through the spring greens, then create four indentations in the vegetables and crack an egg into each one. Season the eggs with a little salt, then return to the oven for a further 10 minutes, until the whites of the eggs are just set.

4. Meanwhile, mix the chilli sauce with the natural yogurt. Serve alongside the eggs and potatoes as soon as they're out of the oven.

RECIPE
PAIRINGS

RECIPE
PAIRINGS

INDIAN FEAST

SPICED ROASTED CARROT & BEAN CURRY (V)	40
BEETROOT, CHICKPEA & COCONUT CURRY (V)	104
CRISPY TAMARIND SPROUTS WITH PEANUTS & SHALLOTS (V)	44
OKRA & CHICKPEA CURRY WITH ALMONDS (V)	75
SIMPLE ALL-IN-ONE DAAL WITH ROASTED SHALLOTS, CORIANDER, POMEGRANATE & CASHEWS (V)	110
SQUASH & SPINACH CURRY (V)	74

SOUTH EAST ASIA

WHOLE ROASTED CABBAGE QUARTERS WITH SICHUAN PEPPER, SESAME & MUSHROOMS (V)	38
SMOKED TOFU WITH FENNEL, PAK CHOI & PEANUT SATAY DRESSING (V)	42
MISO AUBERGINES WITH TOFU, SESAME & CHILLI (V)	66
LIME & CORIANDER MUSHROOMS WITH PAK CHOI & ASPARAGUS (V)	48
GADO GADO: INDONESIAN SALAD WITH WARM POTATOES, GREEN BEANS, BEANSPROUTS & PEANUT-COCONUT DRESSING (V)	94
ALL-IN-ONE STICKY RICE WITH BROCCOLI, SQUASH, CHILLI & GINGER (V)	106

LIGHT LUNCH

LUNCHBOX PASTA SALAD: QUICK ROAST BROCCOLI
WITH OLIVES, SUN-DRIED TOMATOES, BASIL & PINE NUTS (V)   36

ROASTED RED CABBAGE WITH CRISP GARLIC CROUTONS,
APPLE, RAISINS & LAMB'S LETTUCE (V)   34

CARROT & TALEGGIO TARTE TATIN   172

ROSEMARY ROASTED CHICORY & RADISH SALAD
WITH ASPARAGUS & ORANGE (V)   52

MIDDLE EASTERN

ROASTED CAULIFLOWER WITH CHICKPEAS, SPRING GREENS,
LEMON & TAHINI (V)   72

PERSIAN MUSHROOMS WITH POMEGRANATE & WALNUTS (V)   99

WHOLE ROASTED CAULIFLOWER WITH RAS EL HANOUT,
PEARL BARLEY & POMEGRANATE (V)   90

AUBERGINE WITH TOMATOES, HARISSA & ALMONDS (V)   64

ALL-IN-ONE JEWELLED PEARL BARLEY WITH SQUASH,
POMEGRANATE, WATERCRESS & FETA   204

CRISP CAULIFLOWER STEAKS WITH HARISSA & GOAT'S CHEESE   162

RECIPE
PAIRINGS

SOUTH AMERICAN SHARING FEAST

FAJITA SPICED MUSHROOMS & PEPPERS
WITH STILTON & SOUR CREAM   146

THREE BEAN CHILLI WITH AVOCADO SALSA (V)   84

CHIPOTLE ROASTED SWEETCORN
WITH SQUASH, BLACK BEANS, FETA & LIME   194

Note: Make the chilli ahead – the oven will get too steamy
for the sweetcorn to roast if you put them both in at the same time.

AUTUMNAL DINNERS

GENTLY SPICED PEARL BARLEY
WITH TOMATOES, LEEKS, DILL & PINE NUTS (V)   102

SWEET DREAMS ARE MADE OF GREENS (V)   24
  (omit the quinoa)

CREOLE SPICED LEEK & MUSHROOM TART   134

BASIL & THYME ROASTED ONIONS WITH SQUASH,
GOATS CHEESE & WALNUTS   206

WHOLE STUFFED MINI PUMPKINS WITH SAGE & GOAT'S CHEESE   200

QUICK ROASTED FENNEL & BULGUR WHEAT
WITH MOZZARELLA, FIGS, POMEGRANATE & DILL   158

WEEKEND LUNCH

LEEK & PUY LENTIL GRATIN
WITH A CRUNCHY FETA TOPPING   178

WATERCRESS & PARSNIP PANZANELLA
WITH GORGONZOLA, HONEY & RADISHES   176

RED WINE MUSHROOM CASSEROLE
WITH A CHEESE COBBLER TOPPING   190

HONEY ROASTED ROOT VEGETABLE SALAD
WITH BLUE CHEESE & SPINACH   180

SQUASH & GORGONZOLA TART WITH FIGS & PECANS   150

LUX WARM WINTER SALAD: ROASTED POTATOES & CELERIAC
WITH TRUFFLE, PARMESAN & SOFT-BOILED EGGS   213

PICNIC TABLE

THE MOST INDULGENT QUICK COOK QUICHE;
BROCCOLI, GORGONZOLA, CHILLI & WALNUT   130

ROASTED TOMATO, RED PEPPER & ARTICHOKE PANZANELLA
WITH TARRAGON & LEMON   60

HERBY ROASTED PEPPERS STUFFED
WITH ARTICHOKES, OLIVES & FETA   186

RAINBOW TABBOULEH WITH AVOCADO,
RADISHES & POMEGRANATE   30

INDEX

All-in-one jewelled pearl barley with squash,
   pomegranate, watercress & feta 204
All-in-one kale & borlotti minestrone
   with ditalini, chilli oil & pine nuts 92
All-in-one roasted tomato & bay orzo
   with black pepper 28
All-in-one sticky rice with broccoli, squash,
   chilli & ginger 106
All-in-one sweet potato Thai curry 62
almonds
   Aubergine with tomatoes, harissa & almonds 64
   Crispy kale & bulgur wheat salad
      with pomegranates, preserved lemon,
      goat's cheese & almonds 136
   Escalivada: slow roasted peppers, aubergines
      & tomatoes with a basil & almond dressing 88
   Okra & chickpea curry with almonds 75
apples: Roasted red cabbage with crisp garlic
   croutons, apple, raisins & lamb's lettuce 34
artichokes
   Crispy sprout & artichoke gratin
      with lemon & blue cheese 192
   Crunchy roast potato, artichoke
      & spring green hash with baked eggs 218
   Herby roasted peppers stuffed
      with artichokes, olives & feta 186
   Roasted tomato, red pepper & artichoke
      panzanella with tarragon & lemon 60
asparagus
   Caponata style aubergines with olives,
      capers & tomatoes 114
   Courgette, asparagus & goat's cheese tart 140
   Lime & coriander mushrooms with pak choi
      & asparagus 48
   Quick cook leek orzotto with asparagus,
      hazelnuts & rocket 50
   Rosemary roasted chicory & radish salad
      with asparagus & orange 52
   Sweet dreams are made of greens 24
aubergines
   Aubergine & fennel gratin with goat's cheese
      & walnuts 202
   Aubergine with tomatoes, harissa & almonds 64
   Escalivada: slow roasted peppers, aubergines &
      tomatoes with a basil & almond dressing 88
   Miso aubergines with tofu, sesame & chilli 66
   Oven baked ratatouille: slow cooked courgette,
      aubergine, peppers & tomatoes 96
avocado
   Rainbow tabbouleh with avocado, radishes
      & pomegranate 30
   Sweet dreams are made of greens 24
   Three bean chilli with avocado salsa 84

Baked eggs with beetroot, celeriac, dill & feta 144

Basil & thyme roasted onions with squash,
   goat's cheese & walnuts 206
beans
   All-in-one kale & borlotti minestrone
      with ditalini, chilli oil & pine nuts 92
   Cannellini bean falafel with potato wedges,
      spinach & pomegranate 184
   Chipotle roasted sweetcorn with squash,
      black beans, feta & lime 194
   Gado gado: Indonesian salad with warm
      potatoes, green beans, beansprouts
      & peanut-coconut dressing 94
   Green machine: roasted greens with
      ras el hanout, bulgur wheat & ricotta 132
   Herb stuffed roasted onions with cherry
      tomatoes & cannellini beans 212
   Spiced roasted carrot & bean curry 40
   Storecupboard pasta bake: crispy red pepper
      & cannellini beans with gorgonzola 154
   Three bean chilli with avocado salsa 84
beansprouts: Gado gado: Indonesian salad
   with warm potatoes, green beans, beansprouts
   & peanut-coconut dressing 94
beetroot
   Baked eggs with beetroot, celeriac,
      dill & feta 144
   Beetroot, chickpea & coconut curry 104
   Butter roasted harissa leeks & beetroot
      with bulgur wheat & feta 216
bread
   Carrot & kale fattoush 82
   Roasted red cabbage with crisp garlic croutons,
      apple, raisins & lamb's lettuce 34
   Roasted tomato, red pepper & artichoke
      panzanella with tarragon & lemon 60
   Watercress & parsnip panzanella
      with gorgonzola, honey & radishes 176
broccoli
   All-in-one sticky rice with broccoli, squash,
      chilli & ginger 106
   Green machine: roasted greens with
      ras el hanout, bulgur wheat & ricotta 132
   Lunchbox pasta salad: quick-roast broccoli with
      olives, sun-dried tomatoes, basil & pine nuts 36
   Quick cook quiche: broccoli, gorgonzola,
      chilli & walnut 130
   Spicy harissa sprouts & broccoli with halloumi,
      spinach & cous cous 142
Brussels sprouts
   Crispy sprout & artichoke gratin with lemon
      & blue cheese 192
   Crispy tamarind sprouts with peanuts
      & shallots 44
   Spicy harissa sprouts & broccoli with halloumi,
      spinach & cous cous 142

bulgur wheat
    Butter roasted harissa leeks & beetroot
      with bulgur wheat & feta 216
    Crispy kale & bulgur wheat salad
      with pomegranates, preserved lemon,
      goat's cheese & almonds 136
    Green machine: roasted greens with
      ras el hanout, bulgur wheat & ricotta 132
    Quick roasted fennel & bulgur wheat with
      mozzarella, figs, pomegranate & dill 158
    Rainbow tabbouleh with avocado, radishes
      & pomegranate 30
    Side dish 16
  Butter roasted harissa leeks & beetroot
    with bulgur wheat & feta 216

cabbage
    Roasted red cabbage with crisp garlic croutons,
      apple, raisins & lamb's lettuce 34
    Whole roasted cabbage quarters with Sichuan
      pepper, sesame & mushrooms 38
Cannellini bean falafel with potato wedges,
    spinach & pomegranate 184
capers: Caponata style aubergines with olives,
    capers & tomatoes 114
Caponata style aubergines with olives, capers
    & tomatoes 114
carrots
    Carrot & kale fattoush: crisp pitta with spiced
      roasted carrots, kale, dates & lemon 78
    Carrot & taleggio tarte tatin 172
    Honey roasted root vegetable salad with blue
      cheese & spinach 180
    Spiced roasted carrot & bean curry 40
    Wensleydale, parsnip & carrot tart
      with rosemary 182
cashews: Simple all-in-one daal with roasted
    shallots, coriander, pomegranate & cashews 110
cauliflower
    Crisp cauliflower steaks with harissa
      & goat's cheese 162
    Roasted cauliflower with chickpeas,
      spring greens, lemon & tahini 72
    Spiced roasted carrot & bean curry 40
    Whole roasted cauliflower with ras el hanout,
      pearl barley & pomegranate 90
celeriac
    Baked eggs with beetroot, celeriac,
      dill & feta 144
    Honey roasted root vegetable salad
      with blue cheese & spinach 180
    Lux warm winter salad: roasted potatoes
      & celeriac with truffle, parmesan
      & soft-boiled eggs 213

cheese
    Creole spiced leek & mushroom tart 134
    Crispy sprout & artichoke gratin
      with lemon & blue cheese 192
    Honey roasted root vegetable salad
      with blue cheese & spinach 180
    Quick cheese & onion tart 156
    Quick roasted fennel & bulgur wheat
      with mozzarella, figs, pomegranate & dill 158
    Red wine mushroom casserole with a cheese
      cobbler topping 190
    Rich potato & mushroom gratin with cream
      & reblochon 208
    Spicy harissa sprouts & broccoli with halloumi,
      spinach & cous cous 142
    Stuffed roasted fennel & mushrooms
      with Gruyère 188
    Wensleydale, parsnip & carrot tart
      with rosemary 182
    see also: feta; goat's cheese; gorgonzola;
      parmesan; ricotta; stilton; taleggio
chickpeas
    Beetroot, chickpea & coconut curry 104
    Crispy tamarind sprouts with peanuts
      & shallots 44
    Okra & chickpea curry with almonds 75
    Roasted cauliflower with chickpeas,
      spring greens, lemon & tahini 72
chicory: Rosemary roasted chicory & radish salad
    with asparagus & orange 52
chilli
    All-in-one kale & borlotti minestrone
      with ditalini, chilli oil & pine nuts 92
    All-in-one sticky rice with broccoli, squash,
      chilli & ginger 106
    Chipotle roasted sweetcorn with squash,
      black beans, feta & lime 194
    Crispy gnocchi with roasted peppers, chilli,
      rosemary & ricotta 152
    Miso aubergines with tofu, sesame & chilli 66
    Oven baked shakshuka: roasted peppers,
      tomatoes & chilli with eggs 168
    Quick cook quiche: broccoli, gorgonzola,
      chilli & walnut 130
    Three bean chilli with avocado salsa 84
  Chipotle roasted sweetcorn with squash,
    black beans, feta & lime 194
coconut
    All-in-one sweet potato Thai curry 62
    Beetroot, chickpea & coconut curry 104
    Gado gado: Indonesian salad with warm
      potatoes, green beans, beansprouts
      & peanut-coconut dressing 94
    Quick Thai okra with oyster mushrooms
      & coconut milk 32

courgettes
    Courgette, asparagus & goat's cheese tart 140
    Mediterranean courgettes roasted with olives,
        feta & tomatoes 174
    Oven baked ratatouille: slow cooked courgette,
        aubergine, peppers & tomatoes 96
cous cous
    Side dish 16
    Spicy harissa sprouts & broccoli with halloumi,
        spinach & cous cous 142
Creole spiced leek & mushroom tart 134
Crisp cauliflower steaks with harissa
    & goat's cheese 162
Crispy gnocchi with mushrooms, squash & sage 68
Crispy gnocchi with roasted peppers, chilli,
    rosemary & ricotta 152
Crispy kale & bulgur wheat salad
    with pomegranates, preserved lemon,
        goat's cheese & almonds 136
Crispy sprout & artichoke gratin with lemon
    & blue cheese 192
Crispy tamarind sprouts with peanuts
    & shallots 44
Crunchy roast potato, artichoke & spring green
    hash with baked eggs 218
curries
    All-in-one sweet potato Thai curry 62
    Beetroot, chickpea & coconut curry 104
    Okra & chickpea curry with almonds 75
    Simple all-in-one daal with roasted shallots,
        coriander, pomegranate & cashews 110
    Spiced roasted carrot & bean curry 40
    Squash & spinach curry 74

Daal, all-in-one with roasted shallots, coriander,
    pomegranate & cashews 110
dates
    Carrot & kale fattoush: crisp pitta with spiced
        roasted carrots, kale, dates & lemon 78
    Sweet potato & parsnip tagine with dates
        & coriander 98
dressings
    Basil 72
    Basil & almond 92
    Chilli, sesame & lime 66
    Coriander & lime 106
    Dill 102
    Lemon tahini 76
    Lime & soy 48
    Orange 158
    Orange tahini 24
    Peanut satay 42
    Peanut-coconut 94
    Tamarind 44
    Tarragon & lemon 60

eggs
    Baked eggs with beetroot, celeriac,
        dill & feta 144
    Crunchy roast potato, artichoke & spring green
        hash with baked eggs 218
    Lux warm winter salad: roasted potatoes
        & celeriac with truffle, parmesan
        & soft-boiled eggs 213
    Oven baked shakshuka: roasted peppers,
        tomatoes & chilli with eggs 168
Escalivada: slow roasted peppers, aubergines
    & tomatoes with a basil & almond dressing 92

Fajita spiced mushrooms & peppers
    with stilton & sour cream 146
Falafel, cannellini bean with potato wedges,
    spinach & pomegranate 184
faro: Side dish 16
Fattoush, carrot & kale 78
fennel
    Aubergine & fennel gratin with goat's cheese
        & walnuts 202
    Quick roasted fennel & bulgur wheat with
        mozzarella, figs, pomegranate & dill 158
    Smoked tofu with fennel, pak choi & peanut
        satay dressing 42
    Stuffed roasted fennel & mushrooms
        with Gruyère 188
feta
    All-in-one jewelled pearl barley with squash,
        pomegranate, watercress & feta 204
    Baked eggs with beetroot, celeriac,
        dill & feta 144
    Butter roasted harissa leeks & beetroot
        with bulgur wheat & feta 216
    Chipotle roasted sweetcorn with squash,
        black beans, feta & lime 194
    Hasselback squash with roasted onions,
        leeks & feta 203
    Leek & Puy lentil gratin with a crunchy feta
        topping 178
    Mediterranean courgettes roasted with olives,
        feta & tomatoes 174
figs
    Quick roasted fennel & bulgur wheat with
        mozzarella, figs, pomegranate & dill 158
    Squash & gorgonzola tart with figs & pecans 150
Flavour mixes 17

Gado gado: Indonesian salad
    with warm potatoes, green beans, beansprouts
        & peanut-coconut dressing 94
Gently spiced pearl barley with tomatoes, leeks,
    dill & pine nuts 102

gnocchi
  Crispy gnocchi with mushrooms, squash
    & sage 68
  Crispy gnocchi with roasted peppers, chilli,
    rosemary & ricotta 152
goat's cheese
  Aubergine & fennel gratin with goat's cheese
    & walnuts 202
  Basil & thyme roasted onions with squash,
    goat's cheese & walnuts 206
  Courgette, asparagus & goat's cheese tart 140
  Crisp cauliflower steaks with harissa
    & goat's cheese 162
  Crispy kale & bulgur wheat salad
    with pomegranates, preserved lemon,
    goat's cheese & almonds 136
  Herby roasted peppers stuffed with artichokes,
    olives & feta 186
  Whole stuffed mini pumpkins with sage
    & goat's cheese 200
gorgonzola
  Quick cook quiche: broccoli, gorgonzola,
    chilli & walnut 130
  Squash & gorgonzola tart with figs
    & pecans 150
  Storecupboard pasta bake: crispy red pepper
    & cannellini beans with gorgonzola 154
  Watercress & parsnip panzanella with
    gorgonzola, honey & radishes 176
gratins
  Aubergine & fennel gratin with goat's cheese
    & walnuts 202
  Crispy sprout & artichoke gratin with lemon
    & blue cheese 192
  Leek & Puy lentil gratin with a crunchy feta
    topping 178
  Rich potato & mushroom gratin with cream
    & reblochon 208
Green machine: roasted greens with ras el hanout,
  bulgur wheat & ricotta 132
Groundnut stew: sweet potato in a peanut
  & tomato sauce 100
Gruyère: Stuffed roasted fennel & mushrooms
  with Gruyère 188

halloumi: Spicy harissa sprouts & broccoli
  with halloumi, spinach & cous cous 142
harissa
  Aubergine with tomatoes, harissa
    & almonds 64
  Butter roasted harissa leeks & beetroot
    with bulgur wheat & feta 216
  Crisp cauliflower steaks with harissa
    & goat's cheese 162
  Spicy harissa sprouts & broccoli with halloumi,
    spinach & cous cous 142
Hash, crunchy roast potato, artichoke
  & spring green with baked eggs 218
Hasselback squash with roasted onions,
  leeks & feta 203
hazelnuts: Quick cook leek orzotto
  with asparagus, hazelnuts & rocket 50
Herb stuffed roasted onions with cherry tomatoes
  & cannellini beans 212
Herby roasted peppers stuffed with artichokes,
  olives & feta 186
Honey roasted root vegetable salad with blue
  cheese & spinach 180

kale
  All-in-one kale & borlotti minestrone
    with ditalini, chilli oil & pine nuts 92
  Carrot & kale fattoush: crisp pitta with spiced
    roasted carrots, kale, dates & lemon 78
  Crispy kale & bulgur wheat salad
    with pomegranates, preserved lemon,
    goat's cheese & almonds 136

lamb's lettuce
  Carrot & kale fattoush: crisp pitta with spiced
    roasted carrots, kale, dates & lemon 78
  Roasted red cabbage with crisp garlic croutons,
    apple, raisins & lamb's lettuce 34
lentils
  Carrot & kale fattoush 82
  Leek & Puy lentil gratin with a crunchy feta
    topping 178
  Rosemary roasted chicory & radish salad
    with asparagus & orange 52
  Simple all-in-one daal with roasted shallots,
    coriander, pomegranate & cashews 110
Lime & coriander mushrooms with pak choi
  & asparagus 48
Lunchbox pasta salad: quick-roast broccoli with
  olives, sun-dried tomatoes, basil & pine nuts 36
Lux warm winter salad: roasted potatoes
  & celeriac with truffle, parmesan
  & soft-boiled eggs 213

Mediterranean courgettes roasted with olives,
  feta & tomatoes 174
Minestrone, all-in-one kale & borlotti with ditalini,
  chilli oil & pine nuts 92
Miso aubergines with tofu, sesame & chilli 66
Most indulgent quick cook quiche, the: broccoli,
  gorgonzola, chilli & walnut 130
mozzarella: Quick roasted fennel & bulgur wheat
  with mozzarella, figs, pomegranate & dill 158
mushrooms
  Creole spiced leek & mushroom tart 134

Crispy gnocchi with mushrooms, squash
& sage 68
Fajita spiced mushrooms & peppers
with stilton & sour cream 146
Lime & coriander mushrooms with pak choi
& asparagus 48
Persian mushrooms with pomegranate
& walnuts 99
Quick Thai okra with oyster mushrooms
& coconut milk 32
Red wine mushroom casserole with a cheese
cobbler topping 190
Rich potato & mushroom gratin with cream
& reblochon 208
Stuffed roasted fennel & mushrooms
with Gruyère 188
Three bean chilli with avocado salsa 84
Warming sweet potato & mushroom polenta
with tomatoes 108
Whole roasted cabbage quarters with Sichuan
pepper, sesame & mushrooms 38

noodles: All-in-one sweet potato Thai curry 62
nuts see almonds; cashews; hazelnuts; peanuts;
pecans; pine nuts; walnuts

okra
Okra & chickpea curry with almonds 75
Quick Thai okra with oyster mushrooms
& coconut milk 32
olives
Caponata style aubergines with olives,
capers & tomatoes 114
Herby roasted peppers stuffed with artichokes,
olives & feta 186
Lunchbox pasta salad: quick-roast broccoli
with olives, sun-dried tomatoes,
basil & pine nuts 36
Mediterranean courgettes roasted
with olives, feta & tomatoes 174
onions
Basil & thyme roasted onions with squash,
goat's cheese & walnuts 206
Hasselback squash with roasted onions, leeks
& feta 203
Herb stuffed roasted onions with cherry
tomatoes & cannellini beans 212
Quick cheese & onion tart 156
Sweet potato with taleggio, onions & basil 210
orzo see pasta
Oven baked ratatouille: slow cooked courgette,
aubergine, peppers & tomatoes 96
Oven baked shakshuka: roasted peppers,
tomatoes & chilli with eggs 168

pak choi
Lime & coriander mushrooms with pak choi
& asparagus 48
Smoked tofu with fennel, pak choi
& peanut satay dressing 42
panzanella
Roasted tomato, red pepper & artichoke
panzanella with tarragon & lemon 60
Watercress & parsnip panzanella with
gorgonzola, honey & radishes 176
parmesan
Lux warm winter salad: roasted potatoes
& celeriac with truffle, parmesan
& soft-boiled eggs 213
Oven baked ratatouille: slow cooked courgette,
aubergine, peppers & tomatoes 96
parsnips
Honey roasted root vegetable salad
with blue cheese & spinach 180
Sweet potato & parsnip tagine
with dates & coriander 98
Watercress & parsnip panzanella
with gorgonzola, honey & radishes 176
Wensleydale, parsnip & carrot tart
with rosemary 182
pasta
All-in-one roasted tomato & bay orzo
with black pepper 28
All-in-one kale & borlotti minestrone
with ditalini, chilli oil & pine nuts 92
Lunchbox pasta salad: quick-roast broccoli with
olives, sun-dried tomatoes, basil & pine nuts 36
Quick cook leek orzotto with asparagus,
hazelnuts & rocket 50
Side dish 17
Storecupboard pasta bake: crispy red pepper
& cannellini beans with gorgonzola 154
peanuts
Crispy tamarind sprouts with peanuts
& shallots 44
Gado gado: Indonesian salad with warm
potatoes, green beans, beansprouts
& peanut-coconut dressing 94
Groundnut stew: sweet potato in a peanut
& tomato sauce 100
Smoked tofu with fennel, pak choi & peanut
satay dressing 42
pearl barley
All-in-one jewelled pearl barley with squash,
pomegranate, watercress & feta 204
Gently spiced pearl barley with tomatoes, leeks,
dill & pine nuts 102
Side dish 17
Whole roasted cauliflower with ras el hanout,
pearl barley & pomegranate 90

pecans: Squash & gorgonzola tart with figs
& pecans 150
peppers
Crispy gnocchi with roasted peppers,
chilli, rosemary & ricotta 152
Escalivada: slow roasted peppers, aubergines
& tomatoes with a basil & almond dressing 88
Fajita spiced mushrooms & peppers
with stilton & sour cream 146
Herby roasted peppers stuffed with artichokes,
olives & feta 186
Oven baked ratatouille: slow cooked courgette,
aubergine, peppers & tomatoes 96
Oven baked shakshuka: roasted peppers,
tomatoes & chilli with eggs 168
Roasted tomato, red pepper & artichoke
panzanella with tarragon & lemon 60
Storecupboard pasta bake: crispy red pepper
& cannellini beans with gorgonzola 154
Persian mushrooms with pomegranate
& walnuts 99
pine nuts
Gently spiced pearl barley with tomatoes,
leeks, dill & pine nuts 102
Lunchbox pasta salad: quick-roast broccoli
with olives, sun-dried tomatoes,
basil & pine nuts 36
polenta: Warming sweet potato & mushroom
polenta with tomatoes 108
pomegranate
All-in-one jewelled pearl barley with squash,
pomegranate, watercress & feta 204
Cannellini bean falafel with potato wedges,
spinach & pomegranate 184
Crispy kale & bulgur wheat salad
with pomegranates, preserved lemon,
goat's cheese & almonds 136
Persian mushrooms with pomegranate
& walnuts 99
Quick roasted fennel & bulgur wheat with
mozzarella, figs, pomegranate & dill 158
Rainbow tabbouleh with avocado, radishes
& pomegranate 30
Simple all-in-one daal with roasted shallots,
coriander, pomegranate & cashews 110
Whole roasted cauliflower with ras el hanout,
pearl barley & pomegranate 90
potatoes
Cannellini bean falafel with potato wedges,
spinach & pomegranate 184
Crunchy roast potato, artichoke & spring green
hash with baked eggs 218
Gado gado: Indonesian salad with warm
potatoes, green beans, beansprouts
& peanut-coconut dressing 94

Lux warm winter salad: roasted potatoes
& celeriac with truffle, parmesan
& soft-boiled eggs 213
Rich potato & mushroom gratin with cream
& reblochon 208
pumpkins: Whole stuffed mini pumpkins
with sage & goat's cheese 200

Quiche, quick cook: broccoli, gorgonzola, chilli
& walnut 130
Quick cheese & onion tart 156
Quick cook leek orzotto with asparagus,
hazelnuts & rocket 50
Quick cook quiche: broccoli, gorgonzola, chilli
& walnut 130
Quick roasted fennel & bulgur wheat with
mozzarella, figs, pomegranate & dill 158
Quick Thai okra with oyster mushrooms
& coconut milk 32
quinoa
Side dish 16
Sweet dreams are made of greens 24

radishes
Rainbow tabbouleh with avocado, radishes
& pomegranate 30
Rosemary roasted chicory & radish salad
with asparagus & orange 52
Watercress & parsnip panzanella with
gorgonzola, honey & radishes 176
Rainbow tabbouleh with avocado, radishes
& pomegranate 30
Ratatouille, oven baked: slow cooked courgette,
aubergine, peppers & tomatoes 96
reblochon: Rich potato & mushroom gratin
with cream & reblochon 208
Red wine mushroom casserole with a cheese
cobbler topping 190
rice
All-in-one sticky rice with broccoli, squash,
chilli & ginger 106
Side dishes 17
Rich potato & mushroom gratin with cream
& reblochon 208
ricotta
Crispy gnocchi with roasted peppers,
chilli, rosemary & ricotta 152
Green machine: roasted greens with
ras el hanout, bulgur wheat & ricotta 132
Roasted cauliflower with chickpeas, spring greens,
lemon & tahini 72
Roasted red cabbage with crisp garlic croutons,
apple, raisins & lamb's lettuce 34
Roasted tomato, red pepper & artichoke
panzanella with tarragon & lemon 60

rocket: Quick cook leek orzotto with asparagus,
   hazelnuts & rocket 50
Rosemary roasted chicory & radish salad
   with asparagus & orange 52
salads
   Carrot & kale fattoush 82
   Crispy kale & bulgur wheat salad
      with pomegranates, preserved lemon,
      goat's cheese & almonds 136
   Gado gado: Indonesian salad with warm
      potatoes, green beans, beansprouts
      & peanut-coconut dressing 94
   Honey roasted root vegetable salad
      with blue cheese & spinach 180
   Lunchbox pasta salad: quick-roast broccoli
      with olives, sun-dried tomatoes, basil
      & pine nuts 36
   Lux warm winter salad: roasted potatoes
      & celeriac with truffle, parmesan
      & soft-boiled eggs 213
   Roasted red cabbage with crisp garlic
      croutons, apple, raisins & lamb's lettuce 34
   Roasted tomato, red pepper & artichoke
      panzanella with tarragon & lemon 60
   Rosemary roasted chicory & radish salad
      with asparagus & orange 52
   Watercress & parsnip panzanella
      with gorgonzola, honey & radishes 176
Salsa, avocado 88
Scones 190
Shakshuka, oven baked: roasted peppers,
   tomatoes & chilli with eggs 168
shallots
   Crispy tamarind sprouts with peanuts
      & shallots 44
   Simple all-in-one daal with roasted shallots,
      coriander, pomegranate & cashews 110
Sides 16–17
Simple all-in-one daal with roasted shallots,
   coriander, pomegranate & cashews 110
Smoked tofu with fennel, pak choi
   & peanut satay dressing 42
spelt: Side dish 17
Spiced roasted carrot & bean curry 40
Spicy harissa sprouts & broccoli with halloumi,
   spinach & cous cous 142
spinach
   Cannellini bean falafel with potato wedges,
      spinach & pomegranate 184
   Honey roasted root vegetable salad
      with blue cheese & spinach 180
   Spicy harissa sprouts & broccoli with halloumi,
      spinach & cous cous 142
   Squash & spinach curry 74
   Sweet dreams are made of greens 24

spring greens
   Crunchy roast potato, artichoke & spring green
      hash with baked eggs 218
   Green machine: roasted greens
      with ras el hanout, bulgur wheat & ricotta 132
   Miso aubergines with tofu, sesame & chilli 66
   Roasted cauliflower with chickpeas,
      spring greens, lemon & tahini 72
squash
   All-in-one jewelled pearl barley with squash,
      pomegranate, watercress & feta 204
   All-in-one sticky rice with broccoli, squash,
      chilli & ginger 106
   Basil & thyme roasted onions with squash,
      goat's cheese & walnuts 206
   Chipotle roasted sweetcorn with squash,
      black beans, feta & lime 194
   Crispy gnocchi with mushrooms, squash
      & sage 68
   Hasselback squash with roasted onions,
      leeks & feta 203
   Squash & gorgonzola tart with figs
      & pecans 150
   Squash & spinach curry 74
stilton
   Crispy sprout & artichoke gratin with lemon
      & blue cheese 192
   Fajita spiced mushrooms & peppers
      with stilton & sour cream 146
   Honey roasted root vegetable salad
      with blue cheese & spinach 180
Storecupboard pasta bake: crispy red pepper
   & cannellini beans with gorgonzola 154
Stuffed roasted fennel & mushrooms
   with Gruyère 188
Sweet dreams are made of greens 24
sweet potatoes
   All-in-one sweet potato Thai curry 62
   Groundnut stew: sweet potato in a peanut
      & tomato sauce 100
   Sweet potato & parsnip tagine with dates
      & coriander 98
   Sweet potato with taleggio, onions & basil 210
   Warming sweet potato & mushroom polenta
      with tomatoes 108
sweetcorn: chipotle roasted sweetcorn
   with squash, black beans, feta & lime 194

Tabbouleh with avocado, radishes
   & pomegranate 30
Tagine, sweet potato & parsnip with dates
   & coriander 98
tahini
   Roasted cauliflower with chickpeas, spring
      greens, lemon & tahini 72

Sweet dreams are made of greens 24

taleggio
Carrot & taleggio tarte tatin 172
Sweet potato with taleggio, onions & basil 210

tarts
Carrot & taleggio tarte tatin 172
Courgette, asparagus & goat's cheese tart 140
Creole spiced leek & mushroom tart 134
Quick cheese & onion tart 156
Quick cook quiche: broccoli, gorgonzola,
    chilli & walnut 130
Squash & gorgonzola tart with figs
    & pecans 150
Wensleydale, parsnip & carrot tart
    with rosemary 182

Thai curry, all-in-one sweet potato 62

Three bean chilli with avocado salsa 84

tofu
Miso aubergines with tofu, sesame & chilli 66
Smoked tofu with fennel, pak choi
    & peanut satay dressing 42

tomatoes
All-in-one roasted tomato & bay orzo
    with black pepper 28
Aubergine with tomatoes, harissa
    & almonds 64
Caponata style aubergines with olives,
    capers & tomatoes 114
Crispy gnocchi with roasted peppers, chilli,
    rosemary & ricotta 152
Escalivada: slow roasted peppers, aubergines
    & tomatoes with a basil & almond dressing 88
Gently spiced pearl barley with tomatoes,
    leeks, dill & pine nuts 102
Groundnut stew: sweet potato in a peanut
    & tomato sauce 100
Herb stuffed roasted onions with cherry
    tomatoes & cannellini beans 212
Lunchbox pasta salad: quick-roast broccoli
    with olives, sun-dried tomatoes, basil
    & pine nuts 36
Mediterranean courgettes roasted with olives,
    feta & tomatoes 174
Oven baked ratatouille: slow cooked courgette,
    aubergine, peppers & tomatoes 96
Oven baked shakshuka: roasted peppers,
    tomatoes & chilli with eggs 168
Rainbow tabbouleh with avocado, radishes
    & pomegranate 30
Roasted tomato, red pepper & artichoke
    panzanella with tarragon & lemon 60
Three bean chilli with avocado salsa 84
Warming sweet potato & mushroom polenta
    with tomatoes 108

truffles: Lux warm winter salad: roasted potatoes
    & celeriac with truffle, parmesan & soft-boiled
    eggs 213

walnuts
Aubergine & fennel gratin with goat's cheese
    & walnuts 202
Basil & thyme roasted onions with squash,
    goat's cheese & walnuts 206
Persian mushrooms with pomegranate
    & walnuts 99
Quick cook quiche: broccoli, gorgonzola,
    chilli & walnut 130
Warming sweet potato & mushroom polenta
    with tomatoes 108

watercress
All-in-one jewelled pearl barley with squash,
    pomegranate, watercress & feta 204
Watercress & parsnip panzanella with
    gorgonzola, honey & radishes 176

Wensleydale, parsnip & carrot tart
    with rosemary 182

Whole roasted cabbage quarters with Sichuan
    pepper, sesame & mushrooms 38

Whole roasted cauliflower with ras el hanout,
    pearl barley & pomegranate 90

Whole stuffed mini pumpkins with sage
    & goat's cheese 200

Cookbooks are always a collaborative process, and I was delighted to have the same team on this book as for the last. Thanks are owed to Rowan Yapp, Harriet Dobson and the team at Square Peg for taking on another book and for their patience and support throughout the writing and testing, and to Pene Parker for the beautiful design, art direction and help on the shoot. I was incredibly lucky to work with the brilliant David Loftus again on the photographs for the book – thank you so much for making it look wonderful, and for your and Ange's amazing support. Grace Helmer – the illustrations are stunning, thank you so much.

Team Glengyle – what would I do without you? Danielle Adams Norenberg, Christine Beck, Emma Drage and Laura Hutchinson, thank you so much for the thorough recipe testing, advice and general brilliance – I've learned so much from all of you, both in and out of the kitchen.

This sort of cookbook isn't a literary masterpiece (though Alice would approve on account of the many pictures and few words), but I'd like to thank Megan Smedley and Vic Northwood for their early encouragement at a time when it was much needed. It was a privilege to be in your classes, and I was extremely lucky to have you both as teachers.

My family, Parvati, Vijay and Padmini Iyer, are absolutely the best cheerleaders – Ma, thank you so much for your thorough and enthusiastic help recipe testing again; Dad, thank you for your unwavering belief in my abilities; Padz, as tempting as it is to write 'Not you!', Boosh style, you are the best – please can I move into your retirement community? I will do the cooking as long as I don't have to play Gloomhaven.

Ross, the man in my pics – your feedback on every dish in this book was invaluable, from the occasional, slightly pained 'This needs work', through to enthusiastic assent and polished-off plates. Thank you for not minding my kitchen takeover, I know you can't wait to go back to using three saucepans, five steamers, one wok and twelve garlic crushers for every weeknight dinner now that this book is finished. This book is for you.

Rukmini is a food stylist and author of the bestelling
cookbook *The Roasting Tin*. She loves creating new
recipes and working on food photo shoots.
When she's not styling, cooking or entertaining, she
can usually be found reading by the riverside, filling
her balcony and flat with more plants than they
can hold, and planning her dream kitchen garden
complete with pet chickens.

10 9 8 7 6 5 4 3 2 1

Square Peg, an imprint of Vintage,
20 Vauxhall Bridge Road,
London SW1V 2SA

Square Peg is part of the Penguin Random House group of
companies whose addresses can be found at
global.penguinrandomhouse.com.

Penguin
Random House
UK

First published by Square Peg in 2018

Penguin.co.uk/vintage

A CIP catalogue record for this book is available from
the British Library

ISBN 9781910931899

Design by Pene Parker
Photography by David Loftus
Prop styling by Pene Parker
Food styling by Rukmini Iyer
Illustrations by Grace Helmer
Printed and bound by Topan

Penguin Random House is committed to a sustainable future for our
business, our readers and our planet. This book is made from Forest
Stewardship Council® certified paper.